Connecting
80 Surefire Ways to Get What You Say Understood

by

Dr. Walter St. John

RoseDog✿Books

PITTSBURGH, PENNSYLVANIA 15222

RoseDog Books
701 Smithfield Street
Pittsburgh, PA 15222
Visit our website at *www.rosedogbookstore.com*

ISBN: 978-1-4349-3538-0
eISBN: 978-1-4349-3416-1

DEDICATION

This book is dedicated to my parents, Walter Douglas and Frances Elizabeth St. John, who used, and insisted I use, proper speech at all times.

and

Dr. Klonda Lynn, my main speech professor at the University of Arizona for her caring, constant encouragement and infinite patience.

ACKNOWLEDGEMENTS

I am deeply indebted to the hundreds of researchers, writers, and speakers in the field of interpersonal communications whose combined work enabled me to obtain the information I needed for this book.

I am especially grateful to the authors of the communications "classics" for their outstanding contributions to the book:

I also want to recognize the speech faculty at the University of Arizona for all they did to assist me to develop my communications awareness, knowledge and skills. Dr. Klonda Lynn was especially helpful and deserves special recognition.

Janice Gomm typed the manuscript and the Owen Folsom Company generously duplicated copies of the manuscript.

TABLE OF CONTENTS

INTRODUCTION

We have all felt the happiness and satisfaction from getting understood by another person. Conversely, we have felt the frustration and sense of futility when that fails to happen.

Tragically, one of the most difficult challenges we encounter throughout our lives is getting what we say understood. Family members, friends, and business associates all struggle to get what they are saying understood.

Many obstacles exist that interfere with the achievement of mutual understanding. These barriers include differences in: age, gender, race, ethnicity, religion, nationality, culture, occupations, educational levels, beliefs, perceptions, attitudes and intelligence.

Regrettably, despite its importance, the ability to gain understanding between people too often remains only a distant hope rather than a reality.

The purpose of this book is to give you practical and specific ways to connect with people. The ideas presented should help you to say the right things, in the right way at the right time.

The book identifies the major factors that influence a speaker's ability to get understood and explains how he/she can use each of these factors to connect with their listeners.

The suggestions offered are intended to apply whether you are speaking to an individual or group.

The constant and pervasive goal of all communication is to gain mutual understanding. You will enhance your communication if you keep in mind that every message that you send has three components that need to be used effectively: (1) the content, (2) your voice tone and (3) your body language. All three of these elements need to be complementary and consistent with each other if your message is to be interpreted accurately. It is vital that you, as the person speaking, accept the primarily responsibility for getting understood. Here are several points about the organization of this book:

* the content includes eighty separate and distinct factors that influence understanding between the person speaking and person listening. Several of these factors are related and may appear to overlap one another, but they actually contain differences worth noting
* each factor is defined in the first paragraph. Next, an explanation is offered for how such factor should be used to promote understanding
* the information is practical rather than theoretical and is presented with an informal rather than scholarly style
* each topic is offered in a concise manner to save you time.

All topics can be read in short time spurts rather than requiring extended reading time.

The content was carefully researched and gathered from a variety of sources including:

* Training author received while gaining his bachelors degree with a communications major from the University of Arizona and his doctorate with a Counseling minor from the University of Southern California
* Information secured from authors attending post-doctoral workshops conducted by communications authorities

such as: Carl Rogers, Harry Levinson, S.I. Hayakawa, National Training Lab (NTL) staff and <u>Communication Briefings</u> staff

* Notes from University communications courses and seminars taught for twenty some years by the author

* Content from author's various communications publications

* Practical experience as a manager, counselor and family member

* Researching of hundreds of communications books and articles

You definitely have the ability to improve the way you communicate with people.

You can connect with people!

I wish you success in your efforts to connect with people in a mutually rewarding manner.

SECTION 1
PERSONALITY TRAITS

MAKE AN IMPRESSIVE APPEARANCE

"Keep up appearances whatever you do"
- Charles Dickens

Your appearance refers to how you look to others. It is how you view another person outwardly.

Your appearance includes such things as your: dress, grooming, personal hygiene, posture, mannerisms, gestures, and body movements.

Your appearance is extremely important because it tells a great deal about you. People judge you by your appearance. First impressions are especially important and lasting. If you make a bad first impression your listeners may listen to you only half-heartedly or not at all.

Your appearance speaks as well as your voice.

Your clothing sends a message. Strive to dress appropriate to your subject and the occasion. Your dress should never be distracting or call attention to itself. Try to wear what makes you look your best and makes you feel comfortable.

Normally, it is best to dress conservatively and to avoid unconvention fashions. It is important to feel well dressed and yet comfortable with what you are wearing as this bolsters your confidence. To look your best make sure your clothes fit properly and are made with fabrics that look good. Coordinate your colors and wear appropriate shoes. If you wear jewelry choose subdued jewelry in good taste rather than flashy jewelry.

Proper grooming is also important in creating a favorable appearance. Head grooming and hairstyle are especially important. Men should be clean shaven or have a clean neatly trimmed beard. Women should wear the right kind and amount of make up and be certain that it isn't excessive. Shoes are an often overlooked aspect of appearance-they should be clean and polished for both men and women.

The way you hold and move your body helps create a good impression. It is best to stand or sit tall and erect, without appearing stiff. Be careful not to slouch when speaking. Use appropriate gestures and other body movement to supplement what you are saying.

Your mannerisms can either help or hurt your attempt to get understood. Act poised and convey confidence to enhance your credibility and create interest in what you are saying.

Frequent eye contact helps you to project confidence and to obtain feedback from your listeners regarding how what you are saying is being received. Your enthusiasm for your subject can be contagious and encourage your listeners to listen carefully to what you have to say. Animated facial expressions and frequent gestures reinforce the points you are making. And voice variety also helps you to appear enthusiastic.

You help people to be receptive to your comments when you act friendly. By acting friendly you help your listeners to be more responsive and less resistant to your message. You appear more attractive when you smile while speaking. However, it is best not to overdue smiling if the occasion is a serious one. Whenever you smile have a genuine full smile rather than a partial or fleeting smile.

Remember people believe you to really be as you appear to be.

HAVE AN APPEALING
PERSONALITY

"Don't give yourself airs! Do you think I can listen all
day to such stuff? Be off, or I'll kick you downstairs."
- Humpty Dumpty (from Alice in Wonderland)

A person's personality is his/her total behavior and
emotional characteristics. All these characteristics
combined distinguish an individual and group from other
individuals and groups.

YOU ARE YOUR MESSAGE! Your personality is your
most important means of communicating with people as it can
make them receptive to or reject what you say to them.
Therefore, you need to be careful that your personality
enhances rather than detracts from your message. It is
important to realize that sometimes there is so much of the
person in his/her message that their personality interferes with
their message. When this happens your listeners are distracted
and concentrate on the speaker, him or herself, instead of what
they are saying. As the saying goes "How can I hear what you
are saying when there is so much of you saying it?"

It can't be emphasized too much that what matters most
to your listeners is who you are. They are influenced only

second most by how you are saying what you are saying and third most by the content (what) of your message. Yes, it is your speaking style (the how) that is more important to most of your listeners than the substance (the what) of your presentation.

You reveal your personality to people in four ways: (1) your appearance, (2) your choice of words, (3) your voice tone and (4) your body language. Each of these factors is dealt with as separate topics elsewhere in the book.

The following is a list of desirable personality characteristics for speakers to display when speaking to individuals or groups:

* friendly, warm and approachable
* sincere, honest and trustworthy
* genuine, real and authentic
* open-minded, adaptable and flexible
* positive attitude, balanced with a realistic outlook on things
* integrity along with high ethical standards
* enthusiasm for both the topic and listeners
* confident, assured and poised
* modest, unassuming, and down to earth
* candid, straightforward and plain spoken
* sensitive and aware of other peoples' needs and desires
* you (other person centered) rather than I and me centered

CREATE A FEELING OF COMMONALITY

"......... but common interests will always prevail"
- unknown

Commonality refers to relating something familiar or that is known to people generally. It is having something a speaker has in common or shares with his/her listeners.

Your listeners will be more comfortable with you and open to our ideas when your ideas are compatible with their own. People will understand you more when the information you are sharing is consistent with their own beliefs, attitudes and experiences. Therefore, it is imperative that you share the things you have in common with them (and the sooner you do this in your talk the better).

Your goal is to create a sense of unity and togetherness with your listeners. There are an almost endless number of ways that you can do this. These include:

cultural background	ethnic origin	occupations
educational background	nationality	age
life style	leisure time pursuits	interests
language spoken	gender	likes-dislikes

beliefs and attitudes	family	health issues
experiences	regions lived in	problems facing
travel	affiliations	religion

Here are several proven ways that will help you to develop a feeling of commonality with the people you are conversing with:

* stress as many similarities as possible between you and your listeners
* emphasize areas of agreement and downplay areas of disagreement
* strive to agree in principle even if your opinions on the details differ
* use we lots and I, and me little
* preface your statements as follows whenever you can:

1. As we both know
2. As we can both agree
3. We share the same beliefs that ....

* Refer to well known people that are liked and respected by your listeners

* Quote people your listeners know and admire
* Cite local events, situations and examples
* Tell stories of mutual interest
* Use examples closely related to the lives of your listeners
* Demonstrate that you know important things about your listeners
* Smile often and show our listeners you like them and appreciate the opportunity to be with them
* Use words that have a positive impact on people
* Tell something personal about yourself including some mistakes you have made (show that you are human)
* Talk your listener's lingo if it is natural for you to do so (don't talk like you are from Boston when you are talking with people from Atlanta or like a professor when talking with people from humble backgrounds)

DEMONSTRATE THE RIGHT ATTITUDE

"A merry heart doeth good like medicine"
- Proverbs 17:22

One's attitude is his/her predisposition to feel favorably or unfavorably toward a person, object or event.

An attitude can't be observed directly instead it is something that must be inferred from a person's behavior. People convey their attitudes through their appearance, verbal comments, voice tone and body language.

Your attitude is tremendously important because it influences your relations and communications with people. Your attitude can help or hinder your ability to get understood. You need to have the right attitude to communicate anything effectively.

You are in charge of your own attitude and have the option to display either a positive or a negative attitude toward yourself and your listeners as well as the subject you are talking about.

Try to be optimistic about your ability to connect with people. By being optimistic and positive you will help people to feel at ease with you and consequently more receptive to your message.

Mahatma Gandhi made these powerful points re: positive thinking "keep your thoughts positive because your thoughts become your words. Keep your words positive because your words become your behaviors. Keep your behaviors positive because your behaviors become your habits. Keep your habits positive because your habits become your values. Keep your values positive because your values become your destiny."

The following attitudes will assist you to get your message understood by people:

* be friendly and show you like and respect your listeners.
* stress you and we when talking with people and downplay the use of I and me.
* learn something important about your listeners and avoid labeling or stereotyping them.
* be sure to treat your listeners as equals.
* demonstrate confidence balanced with modesty while talking. Sound as though you know what you are talking about without being condescending. Above all avoid coming across as a know it all.
* express yourself simply and use words that are easy to understand.
* be realistic about your listeners knowledge and interest in the subject (neither over or under estimate these.)
* be patient and considerate of your listeners. If they don't understand you right away it is best to refrain from showing any irritation and saying anything critical. Instead, simply state what you want to say in another way.
* expect the best from your listeners and show that you enjoy being with them.
* convey an attitude that you are merely sharing information with your listeners rather than lecturing them.
* show that the important thing is not you but what you are saying. You want to avoid having your listeners ask themselves "How can I hear what you are saying when there is so much of you saying it?"

DESIRE TO GET UNDERSTOOD

"Man's painful desire to communicate without coalescing"
- Clifton Fadiman

A person's desire is his/her wish or want to something. It also means a longing or craving for something.

No one can communicate effectively without the desire to do so. The first step toward getting understood is the desire to be understood.

The desire to be understood requires that you be willing to reveal your true thoughts and feelings about things. Desire also demands that you accept the responsibility for and consequences for anything you disclose. A true desire to get understood also means that you are committed to giving what you say the necessary time and effort to make it comprehensible to people.

The strength of your desire to attain understanding is based on these factors:

1. your views toward the subject-it must be genuinely important to you

2. the occasion itself, is so important that you feel that it is imperative that you get your ideas across accurately

3.   your attitude toward yourself-you need to believe that getting understood is important to your image and reputation

4.   your attitude toward your listeners-you must consider them to be valuable, worthwhile and important people

MAKE A GENUINE EFFORT TO GET UNDERSTOOD

"Keep the faculty of effort alive in you by a little gratuitous exercise every day"
- William James

When you make an effort to get what you say understood you consciously exert energy to do so. Effort involves making a serious and deliberate attempt to get understood.

Getting yourself understood doesn't just happen; it requires desire, strong effort and hard work.

The person speaking is expected to make a concerted effort to get understood. This is his/her responsibility. It is presumptuous to expect your listeners to make a strong effort to understand what you are saying.

You make an effort to get understood by:

* thinking carefully about what you need to say in advance
* learning important things about your listeners ahead of time
* concentrating 100% on what you are saying and blotting out any distractions

---

* having your body language support everything you are saying
* taking the time to adapt your content, wording and speaking style to the people listening to you
* securing feedback from your listeners facial expressions, posture, body movement and questions

BE AWARE OF OTHER PEOPLE

"An unexamined life is not worth living" Socrates

When a person is aware of something he/she is conscious or sensitive to its existence. It is when a person perceives and has knowledge of something.

Your message will be better understood if you can achieve a congruence between how you view things and how your listeners view them. Unless you and your listeners have the same frame of reference misunderstandings are likely to occur. Do your best to imagine how life looks to your listeners so you can adapt what you say and how you say it based on this awareness.

When your awareness is accurate and based on reality you will connect with people better because you can deal with them as they actually are rather than what you mistakenly thought they were.

It is also important to become aware of how you and your subject are perceived by the people listening to you.

Here are several vital things to know regarding awareness that will assist you to get understood:

* your perception of things is based on your: culture, past experiences, self-concept, beliefs, interests, prejudices and mood at a certain time.

* every human being has a unique and different awareness of life, people, objects, and events. No two people see things exactly the same way. As Dr. Konrad Adenauer stated so insightfully: "We will all live under the same sky, but we don't all have the same horizon."

* we are limited in our ability to perceive things. It is simply impossible to be aware of everything. We are able to be aware of only a small part of what exists and is going on and around us.

* our perceptions are selective. We pay attention to certain events, people and information and ignore others. In addition, we tend to see and hear what we expect and want to see and hear (e.g., when listening to presidential debates).

* we tend to tune out information that conflicts with our beliefs and expectations. As Ralph Waldo Emerson so aptly put it "some things have to be believed to be seen"

* one person's reality is pure fantasy to someone else

* since differences in perception are inevitable and so widespread it is important that you avoid making the mistake of assuming that the way you perceive things is accurate and the same as other's view them-it simply ain't so. For example, three people viewing the Grand Canyon might comment thusly:

1. a clergyman "one of the wonders of God"
2. an archaeologist "what a wonder of science"
3. a cowboy "what a heck of a place to lose a cow"

It will help you to understand other people if you become aware of their: ages, gender, educational level, cultural background, personalities, occupations, group affiliations, geographical areas living and lived in, as well as their knowledge, attitudes and interest in the subject being discussed.

You can become aware of important things about people by:

* learning the topics they talk about
* finding out how they spend their time

* asking them questions about themselves
* asking friends and associates about them
* discovering their interests
* noting the things they have strong feelings about
* observing the kinds of words they use
* identifying the groups they are affiliated with
* watching their facial expressions and body language while you are talking with them

FEEL AND SHOW EMPATHY

"We have not really budged a step until we take up
residence in someone else's point of view"
- John Erskine

E mpathetic speakers are aware of and sensitive to the views,
thoughts, feelings, and experiences of their listeners. A
person is empathetic when he/she is free of making judgments
about other people and accepts them for what they are. The
word compassion is often used inter-changeable with empathy.

Understanding is increased when the person speaking and
the person listening have empathy for each other. Mutual
understanding is aided by mutual empathy.

By showing empathy for your listeners you help develop
rapport which further promotes their willingness to try to
understand what you are saying. When a person speaking is
liked he/she create greater receptivity to their messages and thus
his/her listeners try harder to understand what is being said.

You can show your empathy for the thoughts and feelings
of your listeners by:

* finding out what is important to them
* demonstrating you value them as people and consider
them to be important to you

---

* acting friendly and showing that you like them
* using appropriate and respectful words
* talking about things interesting and important to them
* encouraging them to state their ideas and reactions to your comments freely

BE CANDID

"Truth is never pure and rarely simple"
- Oscar Wilde

B eing candid means being sincere and straightforward when you talk with people. It is being free of bias and deception. Synonyms for candid are honesty and frankness.

It is important to realize that the basis for any good relationship is honesty and candid communication.

When being candid you have the choice of being frank and saying something as it exactly is or toning it down some to help your listeners feel more comfortable with what you are saying. It is best to be candid without being brutally frank. It is often quite a challenge to be both frank and tactful at the same time and still get understood. However, it is possible.

You need to let people know exactly what is on your mind in terms they can comprehend. Obviously, people can't guess what is on your mind and what you are really trying to say to them.

Let's be realistic there is risk in saying precisely what you want to say. Frankness can cause the people listening to you to become upset, defensive and even antagonistic toward you.

It is sometimes contrary to your best interests to be completely frank with people because many people become uncomfortable when exposed to the truth or when you call a spade a spade. Therefore, it is foolish to say everything you really want to say and just let the chips fall where they may.

It is best to consider the consequences before simply blurting out completely what is on your mind. It is wise to always use discretion and consider people's feelings when being frank with them. You gain little and can lose a lot from overkill and dumping a full load on people.

On the other hand, you can cause misunderstanding when you are not completely frank with people and sugar coat the truth on important matters. Being politically correct can also cause misunderstanding because it says it as it isn't.

It is a good idea to ask yourself these four questions before being candid with anyone:

1. Why do I need to say what I intend on saying?
2. Do I really need to say it?
3. Will saying it make matters better or worse?
4. How can I say it so clearly that my point gets across and yet tactfully enough to minimize offending the other person?

Here are several tips you can profit from when speaking candidly with people:

* be aware of peoples' need to protect themselves psychologically by using various defense mechanisms such as distorting what you are saying or tuning you out totally
* have the courage to reveal important things about yourself to build trust
* desire to be open and truthful with people
* be willing to accept the consequences of being candid
* trust your listeners to be open to hearing what you have to say
* present the essential facts fairly and objectively
* tell people what you want to talk about and explain why it is necessary
* balance frankness with tact

There are certain words and phrases that you should avoid using because they are the enemies of candor. These include:

* wishy-washy words such as: maybe, appears, perhaps, generally, possibly, and they say
* self-protective disclaimers such as: "just off the top of my head I think" …. or "I don't know if this will work" when you are confident it will or "now this is only a guess but" …
* qualifying words such as "it is my understanding", "it might possibly work", or "don't quote me on this but"

Remember, your goal should be to say things as they really are and not as they are not.

DEMONSTRATE COURAGE

"Courage is a virtue only in proportion as
it is directed by prudence"
- Francpois de la Monta Fenclon

Courage is defined as the moral strength to persevere and withstand danger or fear. A courageous speaker says what needs to be said, says it candidly and directly and then accepts the responsibility for what he/she has said.

There are instances when it requires courage for you to say what needs to be said. Understandably, most people are reluctant at times to say what should be said because they don't want to hurt peoples' feelings or risk being disliked yet, there are situations where you have no choice but to bite the bullet and say what needs to be said.

If you don't say what needs to be said candidly and in a straightforward manner then people can't possibly know what you really mean and thus they will fail to understand what you are saying.

When the situation demands that you level with people and state exactly what needs to be said about something it is wise to first ask yourself these pertinent questions:

* do I really need to say it?
* how can I best say it?

* when is the best time to say it?
* am I the best person to say it?
* what will be the consequences if I say it or or don't say it?

There are unfortunately times when employers, parents, spouses, friends, doctors, clerics, police, counselors and teachers need to deliver bad news or make critical comments to and about people.

Sometimes they have no other options. Here are several examples that require courage to speak frankly with the people involved. (Ask yourself what would be the results of remaining silent, sugar coating your comments or speaking frankly in each instance):

* a doctor having to tell a parent of several young children that he/she has an incurable disease and death is imminent
* an employer informing a worker that he is being laid off when he knows the family is living paycheck to paycheck
* parents telling their young children that they are going to be divorced and the family split up
* a friend telling a close lifelong friend that he/she has bad breath and a repugnant body odor
* a police officer needing to inform a wife that her husband has just been killed in a car wreck

Delaying or failing to say what needs to be said in these situations solves nothing and often makes matters worse. These situations demand that you face the situation courageously and say what needs to be said in a straight forward compassionate manner.

SHOW SINCERITY

"No language but the language of the heart"
- Alexander Pope

To be sincere is to be honest, genuine and heartfelt. There is an absence of hypocrisy, deceit, and subterfuge. A sincere speaker says what he/she honestly thinks, believes and feels about something. He/she share their thoughts fully and candidly without holding anything back when speaking to people.

A speaker's sincerity is important as it is directly related to his/her success when speaking. Sincerity lies at the heart of all communication. To appear sincere you must actually be sincere. It is unwise to fake sincerity because most listeners can quickly detect whether or not you are a person with integrity who is speaking with conviction (talking from your heart and not merely with your lips).

Whenever you are insincere you are sabotaging your speaking efforts because insincere communication is ineffective because it creates resistance to what you are saying.

Your goal as a sincere speaker is to reveal and not conceal. It is to share your thoughts and feelings honestly about a subject rather than to hide or disguise them.

By doing the following you will help project your sincerity to people listening to you.

* speak with conviction-say what you mean, mean what you say and show that you mean it
* be sure your past statements and actions are consistent with what you are currently saying and doing
* know what you are talking about-don't bluff or guess when answering questions. It you don't know the answer to a question simply say "I don't know." Better yet say "I don't know but I will find out for you and get back to you by next week"
* act natural and genuine-avoid putting on airs or displaying any affectation
* smile with a full and lingering smile rather than with a half or fleeting smile
* say the same thing with your words, facial expressions, body movement and voice tone (you need to send a consistent message)
* speak without undue hesitation and without saying anything contradictory
* maintain steady eye contact with your listeners
* avoid having a hidden agenda behind your actual comments

CREATE RAPPORT

"Treat others as they want to be treated,
not as you want to be treated"
- Walter St. John

Rapport exists when harmony is present between people and when they get along well together. It exists when people like and have an affinity for each other.

Rapport is the foundation for all successful relationships and communication. Rapport is to communication what gasoline is to a car. The feelings of your listeners toward you are important in determining their willingness to listen and to understand your message.

People won't try to understand what you are saying unless they like and respect you. If your listeners dislike you, neither your eloquence or style nor your fluency with words will overcome their resistance to your message.

Relational messages exist as well as content messages every time you say something to someone. They demonstrate how the speaker and his/her listeners feel about each other. The closeness of a relationship has a significant impact on how any message is received.

Your relationships will be enhanced if you share your feelings as well as your thoughts with the people you are talking with. Your listeners want to know you as a person in order for them to understand you better.

Your goal when speaking to a single individual or a group of people is to develop as much rapport as you can as quickly as possible. Strive to make your listeners immediately receptive to what you have to say.

These ideas will help you to develop rapport with your listeners:

* find out what your listeners expect from you and tailor your message to meet these expectations
* learn how much your listeners know about the subject
* try to see things from your listeners point of view (let them know you understand their world).
* use the personal touch. Use a lot of personal pronouns (I, we and you). Stress you and we while downplaying I and me when talking with people.
* establish common ground. Emphasize your similarities and minimize your differences. Create a feeling of camaraderie and togetherness
* make your listeners feel important (we all want to feel important and like a somebody)
* show you appreciate yourlisteners' abilities and accomplishments
* involve your listeners-give them a chance to make comments and ask questions. Also ask semi-rhetorical questions to give people an opportunity to respond to what you've said (For example a show of hands)
* cite examples that relate to your listeners daily lives
* build on your listeners pre-existing beliefs and interests
* act enthusiastic and show that you are enjoying yourself. Smile often and big (a smile says I like you and I'm happy to be with you). By smiling you also help your listeners to feel relaxed and comfortable around you
* act modest and down to earth like a regular person
* speak as an equal and play down any differences in status
* act natural and show that you are human

* don't act like a "know it all". Be willing to frankly admit mistakes you've made and state "I don't know" to questions rather than bluffing or guessing with your answers

* speak with a pleasant conversational tone of voice (be sure not to sound preachy or holier than thou)

* show a sense of humor-have fun and laugh with your listeners

* use appealing language. Get on the same wavelength by using familiar words and plain language

* use gender fair and neutral words

ESTABLISH CREDIBILITY

"I hold that the characteristic of the
present age is craving credibility"
- Benjamin Disraeli

Credibility is having the power to gain peoples' trust and belief in what you are saying. To be viewed as credible you need to be seen as trustworthy, competent, sincere and well intentioned.

You must have credibility to be believed. People will pay closer attention to what you are saying when they think that you know what you are talking about. Conversely, without credibility your message will be suspect and may even be discounted. Therefore, it is imperative that you give a top priority to establishing your credibility.

Your reputation precedes the time when you actually begin speaking to people. Your reputation can be an asset or a liability. Ideally your reputation will, by itself, show why you are qualified to speak on the topic. In any event, be sure to tell your listeners about your training and experiences regarding your subject at the start of your talk.

If you are speaking to a large group of people be certain to provide the person assigned to introduce you a succinct list of your most important qualifications for speaking on the topic.

In addition, periodically during your presentation modestly mention additional training and experiences connected to the subject.

Your credibility and overall reputation are enhanced when you are sincere and truthful in all that you say. While speaking you want to show a strong sense of ethics and integrity.

You further aid your credibility and image when you show that you have made a genuine effort to learn important things about your listeners. You will elicit a positive reception from people when you demonstrate that you not only understand their needs and problems but that you share some of them.

Your appearance and mannerisms are important. People will quickly size you up and form an opinion about you before you utter a word. Be sure to wear the appropriate clothing for the occasion and nature of the topic. It is usually best to dress conservatively. Also, look well groomed and refrain from wearing any distracting jewelry.

By looking and acting confident you bolster your credibility. It is essential that you act poised and relaxed in order to appear confident.

You express confidence by dressing appropriately, having an erect posture, maintaining steady eye contact, speaking fluently with an assured manner, gesturing frequently and freely, and by inviting questions. You further exhibit confidence by readily stating you don't know something rather than bluffing and by admitting your past mistakes.

On the other hand, you diminish your projection of confidence when you do the following:

* appear nervous, hesitant and insincere
* act tentative, indecisive and unsure
* make hedging and qualifying statements or habitually using weasel words such as: somewhat, kind of, usually, generally and possibly
* state frequent disclaimers such as "I'm not really sure," "I'm only guessing but…" and "I could be wrong but…"
* have prolonged pauses or repeatedly making sounds such as: ah, em, um, etc.

You further promote your credibility by presenting your information in a logical and well organized sequence.

You create additional trust in your listeners by stating only relevant facts and doing so in a fair and balanced manner (neither under or over stated). Be objective when selecting the information to include in your talk. Verify your facts and cite your sources. Be certain to differentiate between your own personal beliefs and opinions from the actual facts. It is important to note that a single inaccuracy or misrepresentation of facts may jeopardize your credibility.

Your speaking style greatly influences your credibility. Speak enthusiastically and fluently. Pronounce your words correctly, articulate speech sounds clearly, and use proper grammar. Realize that how you say something (style) is typically more important than what you say (substance) to your listeners (people judge you primarily by how you speak rather than by what you say).

Speak in a natural manner-sound like the real you. Talk with a calm low pitched voice with sufficient volume to be heard easily. Also speak in a lively manner with voice variety.

Use language that is in good taste and appropriate to the occasion. Select familiar words that your listeners understand. It is usually best to avoid using technical, fancy and inflated words or slang.

Make sure your body language (facial expressions, posture and gestures) all agree and reinforce the words you are saying (you never want to send mixed messages because these confuse people).

STRIVE TO BE TACTFUL

*"Diplomacy is to do and say the
nastiest things in the nicest way"*
- Isaac Goldberg

Tact is being sensitive to what we say and do in order to maintain good relationships and avoid giving offense to someone. It is saying and doing what is considerate and diplomatic.

Being tactful involves saying and doing the right thing in the right way at the right time. In order to be tactful you need to consider the feelings and viewpoints of other people. In addition, you need to consider the impact and consequences of what you say and do.

One of the realities of life is that the truth hurts sometimes; there is no denying this fact. There are times when you must be candid and say what needs to be said even if it hurts and is distasteful. However, while leveling with someone you need to avoid leveling the person in the process.

The constant challenge is to be tactful even when you have to be "brutally frank." You don't have to be rude to be candid nor lie to be tactful. There is a middle ground. Realize that if you are too tactful or subtle you may fail to convey what you are actually thinking and feeling; therefore your listeners will fail to understand what you are really trying to say.

In order to be tactful people sometimes use euphemisms (saying gentle and soft words to express stronger and harsher feelings). You need to be careful when using euphemisms because they water down or disguise your true feelings on the matter (the result is that what needs to be said does not get said).

Remember your goal when communicating is to speak plainly and candidly without being abrasive, offending people and creating resentment.

You can attain your objective of being tactful by:

* thinking before speaking
* predicting peoples' reactions to what you plan to say and modifying what you are going to say accordingly.
* being polite and respectful with all that you say and do
* treating others as important people and as an equal person
* speaking honestly and candidly without being unpleasant and insulting
* saying negative things in a more gentle and considerate way (euphemistically) yet making sure that your listeners get the point (For example, saying that a person made a mistake rather than stating he/she was wrong to do something)
* using socially acceptable words and avoiding strong and offensive language that unduly antagonizes people (For example, refraining from using profanity or vulgar expressions)
* describing the problem caused by the person rather than blaming or finding fault with the person him/her self
* doing your best to see things from the other person's viewpoint to gain perpective on the situation

BUILD TRUST

"Trust, like the soul, never returns, once it is gone"
- Publilius Syrus

We trust people who talk to us when we have confidence in them and consider them reliable. We have faith that they are telling us the truth.

Effective communication is based on mutual trust. Trust is essential for harmonious relations. Rapport between a speaker and listener contributes greatly to gaining mutual under-standing.

Without a basic trust by listeners toward a speaker they will be reluctant to believe what he/she is saying to them. When trust exists suspicions about a speaker are minimized as is the need for the people listening to act defensive and self-protective.

Any speaker who offends, threatens or diminishes his/her listeners is unlikely to be trusted and thus jeopardizes his/her chances of being understood. Fortunately, there are many ways speakers can gain the trust of their listeners. These include:

* having a reputation of being fair, balanced and objective when presenting information to people
* building a reputation of being a principled person with integrity

* having common goals and interests
* acting open-minded and receptive to new ideas and divergent opinions
* being helpful and cooperative
* following up on promises and honoring commitments
* acting natural and genuine
* revealing something personal about him/herself to show they trust their listeners (trust tends to be a reciprocal act)
* being sincere, truthful and ethical in all that he/she says and does
* showing that he/she understands important things about the listeners
* having their actions match their words
* having words, voice and body language all send the same message
* maintaining steady eye contact
* acting poised, assured and confident when speaking
* acting in a consistent and predictable manner
* demonstrating depth of knowledge concerning the subject and referring to notes only briefly
* providing complete, current and correct information
* citing sources for important information
* being willing to say "I don't know" rather than bluffing or guessing at answers to questions
* admitting past mistakes readily
* using facts and statistics in an objective manner without any attempt to manipulate the data or listeners
* quoting authorities on the subject
* offering solid evidence to support the positions he/she takes on various issues

USE HUMOR CAREFULLY

"Humor is a serious thing. I like to think of it as one
of our greatest and earliest natural resources
that must be preserved at all costs"
- James Thurber

Humor is something designed to be comical, amusing and witty. It includes amusing stories, anecdotes and jokes. Humor is a powerful communications tool that has the ability to make the most boring subject interesting. Humor encourages understanding in several ways:

* gaining and retaining attention and interest
* relieving tension and helping people to relax
* creating a friendly and comfortable climate
* illustrating and developing your subject
* helping to emphasize an important point
* providing a change of pace

Since people have different senses of humor you need to be careful how and when you use it. Discretion is advisable so when in doubt about its appropriateness and how your listeners will react, it is best not to use it.

These suggestions should help you use humor more effectively and therefore increase your listeners understanding:

* use your own natural style of humor (don't work at trying to be funny and don't try to be a comedian)
* make sure your humorous comments are good natured, impersonal and in good taste. For example, it is wise to refrain from sexual, racial, and ethnic stories and jokes.
* limit the number of humorous comments and be brief when making them
* relate your humor to the subject whenever possible
* capitalize on spontaneous opportunities for humor
* use self-depreciating humor because it is especially effective
* minimize your own laughter when saying something funny
* use understatement as a humorous tool
* move on immediately to your next comment if your attempt at humor results in listeners silence or blank stares (don't make comments such as "well I guess that bombed" if your attempt at humor fails)

LISTEN RECIPROCALLY

"If you listen to them you will be listened to"
- William Saroyan

To reciprocate is to have a mutual or equivalent interchange. It is to return in kind. In a communications context it means that after the person who is speaking is finished speaking he/she then listens to what the person who has been listening has to say.

People are more inclined to listen to you and will try harder to understand what you are saying when you reciprocate by listening to them (and showing that you are doing your best to understand them-you need to listen to be heard.)

It is wise not to assume that you understand anything said to you. And it is a good idea to verify anything said to you that you think you may not understand fully (when in doubt find out).

It is also wise to refrain from jumping to conclusions or making premature judgments about either the person speaking or what he/she is saying.

In order to truly listen reciprocally you need a mind set that is more other person centered than self-centered.

There are many ways you can show your listeners that you sincerely want to listen to and understand them. There are two approaches you can take to achieve this: (1) verbally and (2) non-verbally.

Let's first look at the verbal ways you can show that you either understand or are making an effort to understand what the person speaking is saying:

* repeat back, word for word, what has been said to you (mirroring)
* repeat the essence of what was said to you in your own words (paraphrasing)
* ask related follow-up questions about the essence of what you heard
* make related or corresponding comments that build upon what was said
* cite comparable events in your life that are connected to the speaker's remarks
* respond with words that contain the same level or type of feelings as the words used by the person speaking
* use a similar tone of voice to match the tone of the speaker's message
* express interest by saying "would you tell me more about"....
* seek to clarify what was said by comments such as:

1. "this is what I heard you say do I have it right?"
2. "I'm not sure I heard you correctly would you run it by me again?"

* state your reactions to what was said
* give your reasons for agreeing or disagreeing with what you heard
* say reassuring things such as:
"I understand" (with an empathetic look and voice tone)
"I can see why you feel as you do"
"I know, I've been there too"
"I would feel the same way if I were in your place"
"I know what you mean, the same thing happened to me"

Let's now examine several non-verbal things you can do to show you are on the same wavelength and understand the person speaking:

* look directly at the person with an attentive body posture
* have an interested look on your face
* react with facial expressions that are in harmony with what is being said at the time
* nod your head up and down or sideways in response to what is being said
* make sounds that are compatible with what is being said. For example, hm, um, oh, and ah
* remain silent and hear the person out without any interruptions or restless movements of your body
* demonstrate you can do what the speaker talked about or asked you to do

ACT ENTHUSIASTIC

"Nothing great was every achieved without enthusiasm"
- Ralph Waldo Emerson

A n enthusiastic speaker displays excitement, zeal and a strong liking for his/her subject and the opportunity to speak about it.

Enthusiasm is contagious. You need to show that you are enthusiastic about your subject if you expect your listeners to be enthusiastic about it. If your listeners are not excited about the topic and your presentation style they will not be attentive and consequently make little effort to understand what you are saying.

In addition to conveying enthusiasm for your subject you need to show that you like your listeners and are excited about the opportunity to talk with them about it.

You can show your enthusiasm in these ways:

* making a statement about your strong commitment to the subject
* telling about your convictions re: the topic in a manner that reveals your intensity of feeling about the subject
* sharing your personal experiences re: the topic
* demonstrating an extensive knowledge of the subject

* having animated facial expressions while speaking
* using frequent movement and free flowing gestures
* speaking with a lively and expressive voice
* saying some things with a rising voice volume and at a faster rate of speech
* using action language with a punch
* interacting with your listeners in as many ways as possible
* smiling often and showing you are enjoying yourself

GET AND MAINTAIN ATTENTION

"Attention is a hard thing to get from men"
- Francis Bacon

Attention is the readiness of the person listening to hear what the person speaking is saying. Focusing and concentrating are synonyms for attention.

Your first step towards getting understood is gaining and maintaining your listener's attention. No understanding can occur without adequate attention. Strive to get your listeners to concentrate exclusively on what you are saying.

The challenge of securing your listeners attention is a constant one. This is a tremendous challenge because people are bombarded with thousands of messages daily. It is a mistake to assume that people are paying attention to what you are saying just because they are present and looking at you (people are good at faking attention).

People can pay close attention to only one thing at a time. People have short attention spans. They listen in spurts and their mind wanders periodically.

To gain attention you need a strong beginning when talking with people. Your opening comments are extremely important as they are the key to getting people to focus on what you are saying. It is wise to delay your opening statement until your listeners are settled and ready to focus their attention on you. One effective way to begin is by stating your purpose. Another strong beginning is to stress how what you are going to say will benefit your listeners. Answer the question "so what"? immediately. Still another approach is to make a startling statement or to cite a powerful and relevant quotation by someone important to your listeners.

You can also create interest by establishing common ground with your listeners. Reveal something about yourself that connects with your listeners. It helps to make what you are saying relate directly to your listeners lives.

It also helps to establish your credibility immediately. When people know your qualifications for speaking on the topic they will be more inclined to listen to you. A quick summary of your experience, training and expertise on the subject shared in a modest manner will show your listeners why you are worth listening to.

Organize your remarks carefully and logically to maintain your listeners attention. Limit the amount of information you present or you will overwhelm people and they will consequently tune you out.

Your ideas should be organized in a sequence that is easy to follow. Give your main point right away and then number your other main points as you offer them. Carefully show your transitions when going from point to point. Emphasize your key points by pausing or repeating them, and be sure to summarize your main points when ending your talk.

Present your information with an enthusiastic and lively style to gain and maintain attention. Vary your speaking rate and try to speak at between 125-150 words a minute (if you speak too fast or too slow you may lose your listeners attention). Also, change your voice volume and use appropriate gestures to hold people's attention.

It is best to use simple language and words that are familiar to your listeners. Use short words and sentences rather than long ones. Speak in specifics rather than in generalities. Use language that creates mental pictures and visual aids to make your comments more interesting and easy to understand. While using visual aids be sure to look at your listeners and that the visuals are large enough to be seen easily.

Your words should sound spontaneous rather than rehearsed. Use fresh phrases that inject life and color into your language rather than employing trite and tired phrases.

Provide new information and fresh ideas to create interest and maintain attention. Speak about everyday events and real life incidents important to your listeners. Conversely, avoid talking about things people already know and that are common place.

Other things that help you to gain and hold the attention of your listeners include:

* using impressive quotations related to the subject
* asking rhetorical questions to involve people
* employing humor that is in good taste and that is relevant to the point you are making

KNOW AND ACCEPT YOUR
RESPONSIBILITIES AS SPEAKER

"Responsibility is like a string that we can see only
the middle of. Both ends are out of sight."
- William McFee

Responsibility is something that a person is accountable for. It is something a person is answerable for doing. It is a duty or function a person is obligated to fulfill.

The person speaking has the primary responsibility for getting what he/she is saying understood by the people listening. These responsibilities are numerous and almost endless. Conversely, the people listening are only expected to make a reasonable effort to understand what is being said to them.

The major responsibilities are detailed in the various segments of this book and include:

* having a clear purpose and stating this up front to the listeners
* thinking clearly and presenting ones thoughts in an organized and logical sequence
* making a sincere and concerted effort to get understood

* knowing the subject thoroughly and demonstrating competence on the topic
* learning as much about the listeners and their expectations as possible
* establishing rapport and a sense of commonality as quickly as possible
* creating a trusting climate
* using clear, simple, and familiar language when speaking
* speaking with the most effective style for the type of message, occasion and listeners
* providing accurate, complete, and current information in an objective, fair and balanced manner
* adapting the content and language to the people listening
* sending a clear, explicit and consistent message by means of the choice of words, voice tone and body language
* being enthusiastic so that the message will be interesting as well as informative
* emphasizing, summarizing and explaining the main points
* being as brief as possible by limiting the information presented to only the most important and relevant ideas
* using correct grammar and pronouncing words properly
* timing the message for optimal results
* balancing tact with candor when sharing bad news or unwelcome information
* verifying that what you are saying is getting understood by obtaining prompt feedback

It is imperative that the person speaking not only understand these responsibilities but also carry them out to the best of his/her ability.

SECTION 2
ORGANIZING THE MESSAGE

DETERMINE AND STATE
YOUR PURPOSE

"The secret to success is constancy of purpose"
- Benjamin Disraeli

The purpose of a presentation is your goal, aim or objective. It is what you want to achieve as a result of your talk.

Your purpose when speaking is a simple, straight forward and constant one which is to get your listeners to understand what you are saying.

It is imperative that you have a clear understanding of your purpose when you make a presentation. You can't be unclear about your purpose and expect others to be clear about it.

There are two dimensions of purpose to identify:

1. What is my purpose for saying what I am about to say?
2. What is the purpose of my listeners for listening to me?

Ask yourself three key questions to pin down the purpose of your presentation

* what exactly do I want to achieve?
* what specific results do I want?
* what do I want to see happen following my presentation?

After you have carefully considered and decided on your purpose, it is prudent to write it down preferably in one sentence. State your purpose as clearly, specifically and explicitly as possible.

It is a good idea to keep your purpose constantly in mind as you gather material for your talk. Be selective-choose only the material that is most relevant to your purpose.

There are typically three reasons for presenting information to people:

1. to inform them about something important
2. to persuade them to think a certain way
3. to actuate them to do something you want them to do

You have the ethical responsibility to not only have your purpose firmly in your own mind but to share it clearly and candidly with the people listening to you.

It is advisable to state your purpose immediately-don't delay sharing this and forcing your listeners to guess at your purpose. It is also wise to answer these two crucial questions right away for your listeners: (1) how will I benefit from this presentation and (2) what's in it for me?

PREPARE THE CONTENT CAREFULLY

"Practice is the best of all instructors"
- Pubilius Syrus

You prepare for what you are going to say by getting ready ahead of time. You develop and organize your information and work out the details of your presentation.

Careful preparation is required for any effective presentation. You need to organize your information and know your subject thoroughly. It is best to prepare your material so carefully that you can present it extemporaneously rather than reading it.

The first step in preparing your presentation is to determine your purpose. Try to pin down exactly what you want to achieve with your message (what do you specifically want to happen as a result of your message?) After identifying your purpose write it down so that you can refer to it periodically to keep you on course. Limit your purpose statement to as few words as possible.

Next, learn the nature of the occasion, the key information about your listeners, the time available for your talk, and the place where you will be speaking.

The key information you need to know about your listeners includes their:

* attitude and interest in the subject
* knowledge and experience with the subject
* intelligence and educational level
* ages and gender ratios
* occupations
* ethnic and cultural backgrounds
* group affiliations
* expectations regarding your presentation

The third step is to gather data directly related to your purpose and your listeners' knowledge of the subject. Use the most reputable sources when gathering material for your presentation. These sources include:

* library collections
* the internet
* research centers and think tanks
* interviews with authorities on the topic
* your own knowledge and experience with the subject

After identifying the best sources of information, start doing your research. Take notes on the most current, reputable and relevant information. It is wise to accumulate more data than you will be able to use so that you will have an abundance of information to choose from. Check out your facts to make certain they are correct, complete and current.

Next, organize the notes you have taken into three piles (1) must tell, (2) nice to tell time permitting and (3) information to cut.

The next step is to pick out the main ideas along with the supporting data for your main points that you want to present. Normally, it is best to limit your main points to a maximum of five or six (you don't want to overwhelm people with too much information). Supporting material includes: quotations, statistics, relevant stories or anecdotes, examples and visuals to illustrate your points.

After determining your main ideas organize them listing the presentation sequence by developing an outline.

Your outline should contain only key words and phrases rather than complete sentences. After completing your outline take brief notes to use when delivering your talk. It is best to print or type your notes on numbered 3x5 cards that are double or triple spaced. Next, look over your notes to ensure that they make sense (see the topic on notes for more detailed information).

Now that your research is completed, your outline finished and your delivery notes prepared it is time to consider the most effective way to present the different kinds of ideas and facts. It is not enough to know what you want to say: it is also vital that you figure out the best way to say it.

It is now time to practice your presentation aloud using your notes as a guide. It is a good idea to tape or video your practice sessions so that you can get accurate feedback regarding how you sound or look while delivering your talk.

You will need to revise your notes as you deem advisable after each of your practice sessions. Usually, three or four practice sessions should be sufficient. Practice enough to guarantee that you are familiar with your material and yet avoid practicing excessively (your goal is to have your information sound fresh and spontaneous to your listeners).

Pretend that your listeners are present while you are practicing. Glance at your notes only briefly because it is important to maintain steady eye contact with your listeners (you don't want to appear to be reading your notes.)

The last step in your preparation is to check out the place you will be making your presentation ahead of time. Try to conduct your final practice at the same place you will be presenting.

ORGANIZE AND USE YOUR NOTES PROPERLY

"Use notes judiciously, properly and unobtrusively"
- unknown

P resentation notes contain key words or brief comments written on cards or pieces of paper for a speaker to refer to while talking.

There are several important reasons for using notes:

1. helps speaker to remember key points in their proper sequence
2. aids accuracy by listing quotations, statistics, or complicated data so that they can be referred to or read verbatim
3. provides the speaker a sense of security as they serve as a safety valve against forgetting key ideas or their sequence
4. helps to summarize main points at the end of the talk

There are a number of things you can do while preparing and using your notes that will make your presentation more effective. Let's review these.

Preparing of notes:

* write notes on 3x5 white cards or stiff paper (whose pages will not stick together)
* type or print words legibly
* leave plenty of white space between lines of notes (eg. double or triple spaced)
* number each card or piece of paper in the upper right hand corner
* limit notes to key words or short phrases except for quotations and statistics
* emphasize certain words and phrases by underlining, using color or capitalizing them
* put content in the right sequence on notes

Speaking from Notes:
* check to see that the cards or papers are in the proper order before you start
* check out the type of lectern before you begin. For example:

1. Does it have a lip to hold cards or papers?
2. Is there enough light to enable you to see your notes easily?
3. Is the height of the lectern no higher than your waist?
4. Is the height of the lectern such that you can see your notes clearly?

* glance quickly and unobtrusively at your notes rather than studying them and thus drawing your listeners attention to them
* speak from your notes with a natural and flowing style-don't read them except for statistics and quotations
* show you know the material and are free of your notes by maintaining steady eye contact with your listeners (strive for 90% eye contact)

* flip the cards or pages quietly and unobtrusively. Flip them as you come to the end of each page instead of after to maintain the flow of your presentation

* hold 3x5 cards in your hand if your presentation is informal and you want to be able to move around rather than be tied to the lectern

Note if you will be using slides or overhead transparencies during your presentation you can use the key words written on these as your notes rather than relying on your note cards.

MAKE AN EFFECTIVE
INTRODUCTION

"Well begin is half done" anonymous

An introduction is a preliminary statement to the main portion of a presentation. It is your beginning or opening statement that leads into the body of your presentation.

Your introduction is tremendously important to the success of your talk because it sets the tone for the entire presentation. You need to get off to a good start because it is difficult to recover from a bad beginning.

An introduction is used to:

* announce the topic
* state the purpose of your talk
* create interest and gain attention
* inform the people listening about how they will benefit from your comments
* establish your credibility for speaking on the topic
* build good will and establish areas of mutual agreement (commonality)
* preview the main ideas you will be offering
* provide necessary background for the body of your talk

It is wise to keep your introduction brief and simple. It is also advisable to delay choosing the content of your introduction until you have finished organizing your talk.

There are various ways you can introduce a topic such as:

* state the title of your talk and your purpose for speaking about it
* explain the importance of the subject
* state the problem or issue involved
* describe precisely how your listeners will benefit
* cite your personal interest and experience concerning the topic
* refer to people and events of interest to your listeners
* make a startling or controversial statement to grab your listeners attention
* give an overview by summarizing the major points you will be covering
* cite a powerful quotation that is pertinent to the topic
* tell a relevant story or anecdote
* emphasize the importance of the occasion
* define the key technical or specialized terms that are essential for your listeners to understand your comments
* explain complex concepts regarding the essence of your talk
* ask a rhetorical question, or a series of questions, to motivate those listening
* tell a short humorous story that relates to the topic

MAKE AN EFFECTIVE CONCLUSION

"great is the art of beginning, but
greater is the art of ending."
- Henry Wadsworth Longfellow

A conclusion is the closing part of a discourse. It is the ending, completion or finish of a presentation. There are two primary purposes of a conclusion:

1. to let your listeners know you are ending your talk
2. to refresh your listener's memory re: the central theme and the major ideas of your talk

People retain what you say at the beginning and ending of your presentation best. This is why it is imperative that you provide an effective conclusion. A conclusion should be brief and definite, but it should not be sudden or abrupt. It should leave no doubt that you have finished your talk. It is also a good idea to end on a positive and upbeat note.

As is true for the introduction, there are several effective ways you can wrap up your talk. These include:

* summarizing and reinforcing your main ideas
* restating the importance or purpose of your talk
* reviewing how the listeners can benefit from what you've said
* citing a dramatic quotation related to your subject
* issuing a challenge or call to action
* making an emotional appeal
* asking a provocative question for the listeners to ponder
* predicting future events based on the facts you presented
* proposing a specific plan of action
* telling your listeners where they can obtain more information
* announcing the beginning of the question and answer period and how it will be conducted

SECTION 3
CONTENT OF THE MESSAGE

ORGANIZE THE CONTENT

"A bad beginning makes a bad ending" Euripedes

Organized content is arranged into a coherent unity or a functional whole. It is arranged systematically in an orderly sequence.

You need to organize your content if you want to be more easily understood. The first step is organizing what you want to say is to identify your purpose. You need to pin down specifically what you want to achieve with your remarks (then later when making your presentation it is wise to state your purpose right away so your listeners will know what to expect from your message).

After identifying your purpose the next step is to decide on the main points you want to include in your presentation. Next, organize these points into a logical order by developing an outline.

The outline is used to connect and coordinate your main points. It guides your thinking by providing a skeleton of the essence of your message. In addition, the outline separates your main ideas from your subordinate ideas.

Your main points should be directly connected to your purpose. Each main point should be independent of and separate from your other main points. It is best to limit the number of main points so that your listeners will not be overwhelmed with information. By restricting the number of main points you also emphasize their importance. Remember when everything you say is of equal importance nothing is of particular importance.

There are basically five organizational patterns you can choose from. Different subjects require different organizational patterns. You should choose the one that will be the most effective for your subject and listeners The organizational approaches include (1) chronological, (2) topical, (3) spatial, (4) problem and (5) causal.

The chronological approach uses a time order. It presents ideas in the order of their occurrence from the earliest to the latest.

The topical pattern presents information topic by topic according to a logical relationship.

The spatial method organizes content by physical proximity. For example, front to back, top to bottom or closest to furthest.

The problem technique states a problem, analyzes it and then offers possible solutions. And finally, the causal pattern states a cause of something and its results.

To get your ideas understood you need to present them in a logical order that makes sense to your listeners. The order should enable your listeners to make a clear and easy transition in their thinking as you proceed from point to point.

Here are several tips for sequencing your content that will help you to get it understood:

* give your most important points at the beginning and ending of your talk-avoid putting them in the middle where they may be overlooked
* put your main idea first followed by the supporting information
* state simple ideas before complex ones
* present known and familiar information prior to new and unfamiliar information
* offer non-controversial ideas that your listeners agree with before introducing controversial information

* try to learn if your listeners prefer to receive the conclusions (bottom line results) first followed by background information (reasons for the conclusions) or vica-versa.

CREATE AND MAINTAIN PEOPLES' INTEREST

"Talk in terms of your listeners' interests"
- Dale Carnegie

Interest is having a feeling of curiosity, attentiveness or concern about something. The words attention and interest are so closely related that they are often used interchangeably.

People have always faced the challenges of gaining and holding the interest of their listeners. It is presumptuous to assume that just because you are interested in your topic that you listeners are also interested-it just ain't so.

You need to motivate your listeners or they won't listen to you. To motivate them you need to make them feel that their needs and wants will be satisfied by the information you are sharing. Therefore, it is important for you to show immediately how your message will benefit your listeners. You need to answer "so what?" for people to get their attention and keep it.

There are many things you can do to get and keep your listeners interest. These include:

* start with a startling statement that shocks your listeners
* state a dramatic statistic or an impressive quotation connected to your topic

* demonstrate your strong interest in both your topic and your listeners themselves

* explain clearly and specifically why you consider the topic to be so important along with your experience concerning the topic

* refer to people and events that are known to your listeners (For example, local people events and problems.)

* personalize your message and try to involve your listeners as much as you can

* present new and unusual facts related to your topic

* state a controversial opinion

* tell a brief story of special interest to the people

* ask a provocative question and then pause briefly to give people time to mull the question over

* relate a humorous incident that is related to something happening at the time

* speak with a lively enthusiastic manner (vary your voice volume, tone and pitch level)

* talk at a brisk rate and in a confident manner

* speak fluently and smoothly without any awkward pauses

* be listener centered by saying you and we frequently and avoiding the words I, me and my as much as possible

* use fresh words and lively phrases (avoid tired, over used, boring ways of saying things)

* use picture words that create a mental image in your listeners mind

* say things in different ways to avoid sounding repetitive and monotonous

* try to minimize any distractions that compete for your listeners attention

ADAPT THE CONTENT

"What we anticipate seldom occurs: what we
least expect generally happens"
- Benjamin Disraeli

When we adapt our message we adjust it, modify it, and fit it to the particular situation and nature of our listeners.

Since being flexible is basic to getting yourself understood, your ongoing goal should be to be sufficiently flexible so that you can customize your approach as needed. It is important to realize that an approach that aids getting understood by one person may not promote understanding by someone else.

To adapt your message content, wording and speaking style you need to know your listeners and the situation at the time. In order to truly know someone else you need to be other person centered and less self-centered. The frequent use of the word you makes you seem more other person centered whereas the frequent use of the words I and me make you appear to be more self-centered.

Show your listeners you care for them by doing your best to learn what is important to them, their interests goals, ambitions, beliefs, needs, blind spots and touchy areas.

After learning these things about your listeners adapt your message content, word choices and speaking style based on what you have learned.

Your comments should focus on what is important and interesting to your listeners or your message will be less understood or may even be tuned out.

Examples of how to adjust your message to your listeners include:

* if they prefer the conclusions before getting background information use this sequence when presenting information and visa-versa

* if they want to draw their own conclusions from the data you provide then don't state the conclusions

* use examples and explanations that are related to your listeners experiences and backgrounds

* if they like details and plenty of examples and anecdotes present them, if not omit them

* select a setting preferred by your listeners eg. formal or informal

* choose the best day and time of day for your listeners

* adapt the type of content to the knowledge and backgrounds of your listeners

* use a vocabulary level consistent with the educational level of your listeners as well as words that are familiar to them

* use a presentation style based on your listeners preferences

* include a cross-section of your listeners when planning your presentation

* observe the facial expressions and body language of your listeners as you speak and make adjustments based on this feedback

PROVIDE COMPLETE INFORMATION

"Experience is never limited and is never complete"
- Henry James

A complete message contains all the necessary and important information about something-nothing essential is left out. A complete message is thorough,. It is whole rather than partial. A whole message should answer the five W's and one H: who,what,where, when why, and how.

Your goal is to provide your listeners all the information they need without overwhelming them with too much information at one time.

Supply complete information with sufficient details in as few words as possible. You need to offer all significant details to get understood, but not every detail.

When you send only partial messages you create confusion, misunderstanding and even mistrust. When crucial information is left out your listeners will sense that something is missing and wonder what you've omitted and why.

Partial messages can cause problems. When incomplete information is shared the message becomes suspect. And in turn, the sender may lose credibility and the trust of his/her listeners. Additionally, the resulting misunderstanding can result in time and money being wasted.

Identify the essential and non-essential information when preparing your message. Ask yourself "what information is necessary for my listeners to know in order for them to understand what I am saying?"

Begin the preparation of your message by gathering all the data related to your subject. Next, sort the information out and decide which information is essential and which is not. Then, develop your outline listing all of your main points and the sub-points that support your main ideas. Next, revise your outline based on your purpose, nature of the subject and speaking time available. Then, practice your delivery aloud to determine how your ideas connect and whether the content sounds complete and organized to your own ears. The final step is to revise your content based on this assessment.

In the final analysis completeness is measured by how adequate your listeners consider the information you've provided to be.

OFFER RELEVANT INFORMATION

"You learn easier and remember better that which
is interesting and relevant to your life"
- Joseph DeVito

When something is relevant to a person, it is important and significant to him/her. It is pertinent, germane and closely related to the matter being discussed.

To achieve your purpose when speaking you need to gather and present ideas and information that are relevant to your purpose. Conversely, you need to omit any ideas and information that are not pertinent to your goal for speaking.

When presenting it is helpful to ask yourself these questions periodically:

1. Is what I am saying now directly related to my purpose for speaking?
2. Is what I am saying really significant?
3. Does what I am saying really contribute anything or make a difference?

If the answer is no to any of these questions, do not include the material in your talk.

Relevancy has two dimensions:

* it must be relevant in your opinion
* it must be viewed as relevant by the people listening to you.

Realize that a speaker can be interesting, eloquent and enthusiastic and yet say nothing worth listening to. Remember to promote understanding a speaker needs to talk less and say more.

LIMIT THE AMOUNT OF INFORMATION

"Knowledge is of two kinds. We know a subject
ourselves or we know where we can find it"
-Samuel Johnson

Y ou limit the information presented to your listeners by
restricting the quantity or amount of material you offer to
them at any one time.

It is vital that you realize that people can absorb only a
limited amount of information at one time. Brief messages are
not only easier to absorb but emphasize your main points.

The amount of data your listeners can digest depends on
three things:

(1) the complexity of the subject matter
(2) peoples familiarity with the content
(3) their capacity to grasp what you are saying (people
don't want to work hard to figure out what you are saying)

Your goal should be to provide quality not quantity of information. You can limit the information shared if you:

* ask yourself before you say anything "What does what I am about to say have to do with my purpose and how important is it?"
* relate all information directly to your purpose
* stay on track and on target with every comment
* say only what needs to be said then stop
* keep your words and sentences short
* eliminate all irrelevant information to save time even though it may be interesting and entertaining
* spread out important information and offer it in bite-size chunks
* select only information that is compatible with your listeners level of knowledge and sophistication
* take time to get feedback from your listeners on every important point before moving on to the next point

MAKE CONCRETE STATEMENTS

"Prefer the specific to the general, the definite to the
vague and the concrete to the abstract"
- William Strunk and E.B. White

Concrete words refer to specific objects, events, people, material, places and things. They are real and tangible. They can be experienced by the senses (they can be seen-the statue of liberty, they can be heard-symphonic music, they can be touched-a woolen sweater, and they can be smelled-cabbage cooking). A concrete word is the opposite of an abstract word.

Concrete words put otherwise difficult concepts into terms that are familiar and real to people. Tangible words stir up mental associations and stimulate your listeners recalling certain experiences.

The use of some abstract statements is inevitable. However they should be used only when necessary. Abstract words are often meaningless because they are fuzzy and lie outside the experiences of the people listening. Abstractions frequently deal with such intangibles as peoples' feelings, values and beliefs.

The more abstract the word the more ambiguous and difficult it is to understand. Here are a few examples showing how the more fuzzy an abstraction becomes the more difficult it is to understand.

Concrete words:	dollar bill	tomato	catcher
less concrete words:	money	vegetable	baseball player
abstract words:	value	nutrition	athlete

You can make your comments more concrete and less abstract by doing the following:

* before using an abstract word narrow down the concept and find a more concrete term to substitute for it. For example, say Cadillac for luxury car, penicillin for miracle drug, and collie instead of family pet.

* describe the specifics of an actual thing or event. For example: car accident, graduation ceremony, watching a football game

* provide relevant facts and statistics about something. For example, 1.3 trillion dollars instead of massive spending, seven hundred people killed rather than widespread loss of life or forty years old instead of middle aged

* use familiar examples related to the lives of your listeners that create mental images (pictures) in their minds (eg. a rustic rambling farm house surrounded by high grass and birch trees instead of farm house)

PROVIDE ACCURATE INFORMATION

"Some degree of accuracy must be
sacrificed to conciseness"
- Samuel Johnson

An accurate message is correct, truthful and free from error. Accurate information is objective, balanced and factual. In addition it is valid, reliable and complete.

In order to get understood you need to use words both accurately and correctly.

It is important to recognize the affect of the accuracy of your message on your credibility and how your message is understood. It is also important to be aware of the favorable and unfavorable feelings that certain words and information can arouse in your listeners because these feelings can influence the accuracy of your listeners interpretation of what you are saying.

The correctness of your information can be no better than the related facts you have gathered on the topic.

To avoid sharing inaccurate information you need to avoid hit and miss or slanted ways of gathering information. A recommended approach is as follows:

1. Collect all the pertinent information on the topic.
2. Verify the correctness, timeliness and completeness of the data you collect.
3. Separate the facts gathered from opinions, beliefs and inferences.
4. Discard all but the factual data.
5. Analyze the facts to get them straight (understood) in your own mind.
6. Use only the best of the remaining information.

It is essential that you ask yourself whether the information you are going to convey is based on facts, inferences, opinions or value judgments. Here is an example to help you to differentiate among these factors.

1. Fact-the car is black. Black cars get hot because they draw more heat from the sun.
2. Opinion-white cars are better than black cars.
3. Value judgment-I don't like to be hot so I don't like black cars.
4. Inference-since black cars are hot all cars irrespective of color are hot.

In the event that you give out some incorrect information or sense it has been misunderstood, immediately try to remedy the situation by saying something like this, "sorry, hold on, what I said did not come out right let me state it in a different way".

Remember when talking with people that your constant goal is to share accurate information at all times.

SEND A CONSISTENT MESSAGE

"A foolish consistency is the hobgoblin of little minds"
- Ralph Waldo Emerson

A consistent message is marked by harmony, coherence, and compatibility. All parts of the message hang together in a unified manner. There is an absence of conflicting and contradictory information.

Your verbal and non-verbal messages need to be consistent or misunderstanding will result. Whenever your words and body language are inconsistent you send mixed messages to your listeners; (when this happens most people believe that your body language is conveying the true message).

These tips should help you to send consistent messages:

* be aware of what your words and body language are communicating to people
* make sure that your words and body language (facial expressions, posture, gestures and movement) agree with each other and are transmitting the same message
* have your appearance and language be consistent with and appropriate for the occasion, subject matter, and listeners' expectations

* be certain that your content and style of delivery are complementary. For example, a serious topic requires a serious business like presentation style

* convey information that is clear and non-contradictory. The points you are presenting need to agree with each other and be mutually supportive of your overall goal

* use grammar that is proper and consistent. For example, (1) subject and verb should agree, (2) nouns and pronouns need to agree and your tenses should agree

* strive to have your words, voice tone, voice volume, rate of speaking, facial expressions and body language all say the same thing at the same time

The best way to develop trust and thus promote understanding is to be consistent in what you are saying and how you are saying it

SECTION 4
CONTEXT OF A MESSAGE

CONSIDER THE CONTEXT CAREFULLY

"In addition to analyzing specific listeners, you will have to devote some attention to the specific context in which you speak"
- Joseph Devito

Context is the weaving together of words or parts of a discussion that surround a word or passage that can throw light on its meaning. Context is also the inter-related conditions in which your speaking occurs.

Context includes such factors as:

people involved	timing	preceedings and following events
communications climate	location	distracting noise and activity
the situation	the occasion	seating arrangement
related information received	listeners knowledge	expectations of listeners

Context is tremendously important in giving meaning to words. It determines the sense in which a word is used and interpreted. The full meaning of a word can't be understood until it is placed in a certain context. The same word can mean different things to different people in different situations. Here are several examples to illustrate how the meaning of words varies depending on their context:

* A woman whispers seductively "I hate you" into the ear of her lover as they cuddle.
* A New Englander says it is snowing to an Eskimo and receives a blank stare because Eskimos have many words that are used to show gradients for different kinds of snow. Consequently, one word for snow doesn't really communicate anything to them.
* A watch maker views one inch as a large measurement whereas a bull dozer operator perceives one inch as being miniscule.
* A person from Florida may comment "It sure is cold today." when the temperature is fifty while a resident of Maine may remark "It is rather warm today when they are at the same place."
* The word soon often means something different to a Hispanic person than it does to a person with Anglo-Saxon heritage because of the difference in their cultures.

It is also worth noting that the same word can have many meanings. For example, the word set has over two hundred meanings and can have different meanings in different contexts. For example, A set of China, set the flowers over there, he won in the final set of tennis. The words run and cat also have many different meanings.

Understanding is frequently affected by the feelings that certain words evoke. For example:

* the word union is viewed favorably by factory workers and with disdain by many people with management positions
* the word police is perceived differently by people living in a dictatorship from those living in a democracy

* the word liberal is viewed differently by democrats than by republicans

* the word hunger has a different meaning to the people in Haiti than it does to most Americans

These examples demonstrate how strongly context influences meaning and emphasizes the need to consider context when you are talking about important matters.

It is imperative that you consider the many contexts of a word if you want to get your message understood.

UNDERSTAND YOUR LISTENER'S CULTURE

"The greatest law of culture: let each become all
that he was created capable of being"
- Thomas Carlyle

A culture is the customary beliefs, social forms and material traits of a racial, ethnic, religious or particular group of people. Our culture tells us what to believe as well as how to think and act.

In order to communicate effectively you need to understand and appreciate cultural diversity. You need to adapt your communications, attitudes, style and language to your listener's culture. It would be naive to expect that members of different cultures will interpret what they hear in the same way. It would be equally naive to expect that an acceptable way of communicating in one culture would also be acceptable in another culture.

Each of us has his/her own unique culture. No two cultures are alike. However, some are more similar and dissimilar than others.

The cultural differences of your listeners are important for you to be aware of when you are organizing and delivering a talk whether to a group or a single individual. Important cultural differences that can cause misunderstanding include:

gender	religious	educational level
age	social class	type of occupation
racial	regional	nationality
ethic	spoken language	political affiliations

Let's look at several examples of how cultural differences affect communication and getting understood:

1. Gender
    Men and women communicate differently. Men tend to dominate conversations and to interrupt more often than women. Men usually say things in a more direct, frank and let the chips fall where they may manner. Whereas, women are more sensitive and talk more about their feelings. In addition, women generally state things more indirectly and delicately.

2. Ethnic and Racial
    People of different racial and ethnic backgrounds vary in how direct and indirect they say things, the formality or informality of their style of speaking, how they express agreement and disagreement and their use of body language (e.g. Japanese-Americans).

3. Religious
    Some religious impact more deeply on their peoples' daily lives. Some emphasize the past, some the present and others the future to a greater extent and they define the roles of family members differently (e.g. Muslims-Christians).

4. Regional
    Traditions, customs and lifestyle vary in different regions of a country. Some use standard American speech and pronunciation, whereas, others have unique dialects and use frequent colloquialisms when speaking. Also the types of

occupations, political and religious beliefs may vary considerably (e.g. deep south-New England).

5. Language Use

People prefer to speak in their own language, to say and hear words that they are familiar and that they are comfortable with. It is important to realizes that words in one language do not always have an equivalent meaning in another language. In fact, the meaning of words can differ even within the same country.

6. Voice

Speaking with a loud voice is acceptable in some cultures and resented in others. A friendly informal speaking style may be viewed as appropriate in some cultures and inappropriate and rude in others (e.g. British-Americans).

7. Body Language

Frequent and steady eye contact is viewed favorably in certain cultures and unfavorably in others. The meaning of various body movements and gestures is also interpreted differently. For example, in some cultures nodding the head up and down means no. And perfectly innocent gestures by the people in one culture are perceived as obscene and rude in others. For example, showing the soles of one's shoes to the person you are conversing with in Japan.

8. Space

Standing or sitting close to another person while speaking is comfortable and desirable by people in some cultures. Conversely, people from other cultures find such closeness to be objectionable and distasteful (e.g. Hispanics-Anglosaxons).

9. Time

Various cultures perceive time differently. For example, some emphasizes the future and project a sense of urgency and others the past with no sense of the immediate when conversing. (For example, people with a northern European background versus people with a Hispanic heritage or Asian-United States).

10. Colors and Numbers

Even numbers and colors can cause communications problems. In some cultures certain numbers and colors are associated with good luck and viewed positively. However, in other cultures these are not important factors to consider when communicating. (e.g. 7 considered good luck and 13 bad luck by Americans whereas other nations believe other numbers are good and bad luck).

You can improve your chances of getting understood by people from different cultures by doing the following:

* observing how the members of various cultures communicate with each other-especially their use of body language
* learning the cultural backgrounds of your listeners and adapting your content, organization and delivery accordingly
* showing that you accept and understand the particular culture of your listeners (however be careful not to stereotype any group of people)
* pronouncing names and places that relate to other cultures correctly
* being patient and diplomatic when speaking and listening-don't show any frustration or irritation when what you are saying doesn't appear to be getting across
* speaking slowly, distinctly and loudly enough to be easily understood (avoid merely talking louder or just repeating the same words in an effort to get understood better)
* using simple words that are familiar to your listeners (refrain from using slang, idioms, acronyms and technical terms)
* limiting sentences to one idea and using short words and sentences when saying something
* being as clear and explicit as possible (avoid implications and subtley)

* matching the rate of your speaking to the type of content and the backgrounds of your listeners

* emphasizing and summarizing the key information

* citing frequent examples

* using words that create mental imagers for people (showing visuals will help you to do this)

* being sure your facial expressions, gestures and body movements are appropriate and don't offend people

* obtain frequent feedback by watching body language and asking questions

HAVE REALISTIC EXPECTATIONS

"The quality of our expectations determines
the quality of our actions"
- Andr´e Godin

When a person expects something he/she awaits it, looks forward to it and anticipates it,.

You can expect to be misunderstood by some people some of the time about something. It is important to realize that the 100% of transfer of meaning is impossible. No communication is ever exact rather communication between people is always an approximation of what the speaker meant to convey compared with how the listeners interpret what was said.

Expect to work hard to get understood. You can expect that you will need to learn important things about your listeners in order to get understood. For example, their backgrounds, interests in the subject, ages, gender mix, and occupations. After making this assessment expect to adapt your message content, and your speaking style accordingly.

Both the person speaking and his/her listeners have certain expectations regarding the presentation and if these expectations are not met communication suffers.

Here are several expectations that affect a speaker's ability to get understood:

* amount of agreement on the purpose and importance of the presentation

* that your listeners will be preoccupied with their own thoughts and you will need to work to get and maintain their attention

* that the listeners interest in you and your topic will vary and will waiver from time to time as you speak so you will need to find effective ways to motivate them

* that your listeners ability to understand what you are saying will differ and thus you will need to strike a balance between talking at either too high or too low a level conceptually

* that your style, or way of speaking, will be more important in your struggle to get understood than the substance of your talk

* that periodically you will need to slow down your rate of speaking, or even pause, to let your listeners digest what you've said and for you to obtain feedback

* that you will need to adapt your language to the type of listeners

* that your listeners attitudes and emotions about the things you say will interfere with their ability to listen to you objectively

* that you will need to be liked, or at least respected, by your listeners for them to receive your message favorably

CREATE THE RIGHT SETTING

"Always seek the best place to make a presentation"
- anonymous

The setting is the place or venue where you will be speaking. It is the speaking environment.

It is important to control the environment where you will be speaking. The setting, by itself, can make or break your presentation.

The speaking environment includes such things as:

* appearance (attractiveness) of room
* temperature of room
* ventilation of room
* lighting in room
* acoustics of room
* size and shape of room
* seating arrangement
* stationary or movable chairs-tables
* length of time room is available
* noise level of surrounding areas
* distractions in area
* tables available for equipment, handouts, etc.
* lighting adjustability

* instructional equipment available
* secure storage areas nearby
* presence of rest rooms and water fountains
* food and snacks available
* locations for serving of meals

You will enhance your chances of making an effective presentation if you do the following regarding the place you will be speaking:

* look over the presentation spot in advance to familiarize yourself with it so that you can make any necessary adjustments
* conduct your final practice on-site in the same area you will be speaking
* test all equipment you will be using (visual aids, lighting, microphones and the lectern height) in advance to ensure everything is in working order
* have back up equipment readily available
* locate electrical outlets and request extension cords if needed
* pick a place as free of distracting activity and competing noise as possible (For example, avoid being next to a kitchen, a rest room, busy outside traffic, a swimming pool with people parading by in swimming suits and noisy corridors)
* announce times of breaks and meals s well as locations of telephones, rest rooms and water fountains at the start of your presentation
* take room phones off the hook so you won't be interrupted by their ringing
* request that the people present shut off their cell phones throughout your talk

PROVIDE SUFFICIENT TIME

*"There is a right time and a wrong time
to say and do everything"*
- Walter St. John

Time is a measurable period or duration during which an action, process or condition exists or continues. The goal is to allocate adequate time to get what you want to say said clearly and understood.

Select the best time, for both you and your listeners to discuss an important matter or to share bad news (these times are cited, in the following timing topics).

It is essential that you organize your time use. The importance and amount of content of a topic determines the time needed to discuss the subject sufficiently. The opposite is also true- the time available limits the amount of information that you can convey at one time. Therefore, time available and the amount of information you want to present need to be properly balanced.

Give important information more time and unimportant information less time. You need to allocate more time to the important content in order to emphasize and clarify it. The amount of time devoted to each main topic depends on the amount and complexity of the supporting information for each of the main topics. Allocate sufficient time to each main topic but be careful not to provide an excessive amount for any one topic.

It is a mistake to offer too much information in too little time. You need to be discriminating and limit the amount of information to be shared based on the time available.

Generally, a presentation should not exceed one hour. It is a good idea to limit your speaking to a maximum of forty minutes and the question and answer period to twenty minutes (most listeners' attention begins to fade after twenty minutes or so).

It is best to start preparing early for a presentation to a group (preferably one to two weeks). Allow yourself plenty of time to collect, screen, and organize your data as well as to practice your talk.

When organizing your data it is a good idea to organize it in a chronological order that follow the sequence of events as they occurred.

Respect and honor the time limits for your presentation. Start on time and end on time! Begin with a short introduction, speak at a rate of 120-150 words a minute. State important information more slowly than lesser important information (stop promptly when finished- don't drag it out).

Time your presentation when practicing (be sure to practice aloud). Time not only your total presentation but each of the major topics separately so that you can analyze your time allocations and adjust them as needed (it helps to use a watch or clock with a second hand).

Keep continuous track of the time while making your presentation. Time has a way of getting away from speakers before they know it.

Place your watch and a card with the ending time on the lectern where you can see them easily and frequently. By checking your watch or a clock periodically you can be fully aware of how you are doing time wise (don't just guess about the time remaining).

You want to avoid the pitfall of suddenly realizing that your time is almost up and that you still have several important things to say. Also, avoid the temptation to speed up the end of your presentation and thus cause your listeners to feel rushed and overwhelmed.

These tips should enable you to make efficient use of time:

* Determine the exact purpose of your presentation. Take time to consider the key things you want to say and how to best say them
* Learn crucial facts about your listeners
* Pilot test your talk with people representative of the group you will be addressing. Revise the content based on this feedback.
* Predict the possible reactions to your remarks so that you can deal with them proactively
* Build rapport and establish your credibility at the beginning of your remarks (be brief)
* Select the best wording to get your ideas across before you say anything of consequence
* Consider how much time people need to absorb what you have told them- pause accordingly
* Get ongoing feedback to clarify any misunderstandings (seek it immediately when people look confused)
* Pause to emphasize key points
* Repeat important ideas several times to reinforce them
* Show clear transitions when you go from one idea to the next
* Respond to questions during your talk at appropriate times (usually immediately after you have completed your thought)
* Repeat all of the questions asked during the question and answer period
* Pause briefly after being asked a question during the Q and A period to make sure you understand the question and to give you time to consider your answer

You can save time by doing these things:

* Defining and narrowing the purpose of your presentation
* Identifying and limiting the number of major topics and the supporting information for each

* Providing sufficient advance notice to people re: the time, place and topic

* Sending necessary background information a few days ahead of time so people can become more knowledgeable and better prepared

* Cutting out any unnecessary information and words that add nothing to the discourse

* Eliminating time consuming words and sounds such as these that waste time: uh, er. um. you know, saying okay at the end of sentences and using empty phrases such as and stuff like that

* Avoiding rambling comments by the speaker and irrelevant remarks by the listeners

* Using unrelated humor sparingly. For example, telling long involved jokes

* Remaining standing while conversing with individuals and small groups

* Using visuals only when they clarify information and offer it in a concise manner

It is worth noting that you can often say more with fewer words thus guaranteeing that you have sufficient time for your presentation.

SELECT THE BEST TIMING FOR LARGE GROUPS

"Dost thou love life? then do not squander time,
for that's the stuff life is made of"
-Benjamin Franklin

The time available for speakers to make their presentation is the number of minutes that they have at their disposal for their presentation (including the question and answer period).

It is vital that a speaker know the total time available for his/her presentation. Most speaking occasions have two aspects (1) speaking time and (2) question and answer time. The recommended ratio between these is a minimum of 3-1. For example, if the time available is sixty minutes, forty-five would be allocated to speaking and fifteen to the Q and A period. The maximum ratio is 2-1 or forty minutes for speaking and twenty minutes for the question and answer period.

The times of day and day of the week that you are scheduled to make your presentation greatly influence the success of your presentation. The best times of the day are mid-morning (eg. 10 o'clock), mid-afternoon (eg. 2 o'clock) or mid-evening (eg. 8 o'clock). If you are scheduled too early in the morning your listeners may not be fully awake or arrive on-site late. If it is scheduled shortly before lunch your listeners attention may be divided between your talk and thinking about lunch. If your talk is slated to be soon after lunch your listeners may feel sleepy or lethargic. If your presentation is scheduled for late afternoon your listeners are likely to feel tired, pre-occupied with dinner plans, or leaving for home. If it is scheduled too early in the evening people may need to rush their meal, or may not have time to unwind from the days work. And if it is to be held late evening your listeners may feel tired or sleepy. Mid-week (Tuesday through Thursday) are the best days to make an important presentation. Try to avoid Mondays and Fridays. People like to concentrate on their job on Mondays especially in the morning so they can get their week off to a good start. In addition, they may need some "recovery" time from a busy weekend.

Fridays should also be avoided because people tend to be preoccupied with either wrapping up their weeks work or their plans for the weekend. Also, by Friday many people are exhausted and find it difficult to concentrate on new or complicated information.

Practice is mandatory if you want to time your presentation accurately. Your practice should be aloud, standing up and employ the same presentation style you plan to use for the actual presentation (For example, extemporaneous, or to be read from a manuscript or teleprompter).

It is a good idea to time each major segment of your talk separately. This allows you to proportion your time optimally for each of your main topics. It is also recommended that you time each practice session because they will differ.

It is rare that the practice time and presentation time end up being exactly the same. This is to be expected. If your presentation time takes a little less time than planned you can simply stop and go immediately into the Q and A period. In the event your presentation requires considerably less time than allocated (not likely to happen) you should have some filler information available to consume the extra time.

On the other hand, if your delivery runs more than a couple of minutes more than time allocated, it is wise to have some throw away material toward the end of the talk. By cutting out this non-essential information you can stay on schedule without causing a problem.

Time limits should be faithfully adhered to especially if there is a full program with several people scheduled to speak. It is only a minor problem if you speak too briefly, however, it is a major problem if you speak too long.

It is wise to have a watch available to glance at in the event there is no wall clock in the room that can be easily seen from the speakers position. When looking at a clock or your watch be sure to do this quickly and unobtrusively so that you don't distract your listeners. It is also helpful to write down your ending time and place it where you can see it readily to serve as a reminder of when you need to stop speaking.

Unless you are speaking on radio or television, going over or under your time limit by a couple of minutes should not be a major concern.

CHOOSE THE BEST TIMING
FOR INDIVIDUALS AND
SMALL GROUPS

"He knew the precise psychological
moment to say nothing"
- Oscar Wilde

Timing involves the selection for maximum effect of the precise moment for beginning or ending something. Optimal timing is doing something at just the right moment to get the best results.

Timing is vital to the success of any message. The events immediately preceding and following the time you are scheduled to talk with an individual or small group have a tremendous affect on how your message is received.

It is crucial to give people advance notice regarding anything important. If information is not received when it is expected your listeners may object to its lateness and be less receptive to it. People need to receive information in time to act on it properly. When you give people out of date information it is often as bad or worse than not giving it at all.

In addition, be sure to allow plenty of time for sharing information that is new or hard to understand so that the people hearing it have sufficient time to absorb and discuss it (it is never wise to share important information in a rushed manner).

Select the best time to share ideas for both you and your listeners if you want to get the best results.

The best times to talk with an individual or small group are:

* when it is mutually convenient'
* when neither you nor your listeners are preoccupied
* when your listeners are free of stress
* when the information is both current and complete
* when both you and others are relaxed and in a good mood
* when you can have an uninterrupted discussion free of distractions
* when you and your listeners are feeling well and energized

Just as there are best times to talk with people about significant matters there are worst times such as:

* when either you or your listeners are tired or sick
* when either you or your listeners are stressed or upset
* when it is early or late in the day
* when either you or your listeners have just finished a big meal or are feeling hungry
* when your listeners have just received bad news
* when either you or your listeners are in a bad mood or angry with one another
* when you have inadequate time to think about what you want to say or would have to rush saying it
* when major changes have occurred in the lives of your listeners such as new jobs or responsibilities, being laid off or fired
* when the listeners are about to go on vacation or have just returned from one and are busy catching up on their work

* when listeners are planning or involved with holiday activities

This final thought is worth noting. It is easy to say the wrong things when rushed, it is also easy to say the right thing in the wrong way. Furthermore, it is easy to say the right thing in the right way at the wrong time.

SECTION 5
WORD AND LANGUAGE USE

DEVELOP AN EXTENSIVE VOCABULARY

"'Tis what I feel, but can't define, tis what
I know, but can't express"
- Beilby Porteus

A person's vocabulary is the sum and variety of words he/she has available to use when speaking or writing.

The bigger your vocabulary the better. By having an extensive vocabulary you are able to choose the exact words that best say what you want to say about something. The use of precise language is required for a person to get understood optimally.

Generally, it is advisable to use short simple words and plain easy to understand language rather than long words and fancy language. However, it is permissible to use long words when they most precisely express what you are thinking and feeling. The fact is that sometimes there are no satisfactory substitute or alternate words to select from (For example, specialized fields such as science and medicine.)

Standard or commonly used words communicate best. Your listeners must be able to understand the words you use or there will be a communications breakdown. Therefore, it is wise to refrain from using slang, idioms, foreign words, and long unfamiliar words and phrases.

The backgrounds, educational level and intellectual abilities of your listeners limit the level of vocabulary you can use. If you use a high level vocabulary your uneducated listeners won't understand you. Conversely, if you use a low level vocabulary you are likely to offend your educated listeners. In these instances you will be either talking over the heads of people or talking down to them. In either case you risk being misunderstood and may even antagonize people.

It is essential that you say words familiar to your listeners. Also, be sure that the words you use have the same basic meaning for both you and your listeners. Beware of assuming you are being understood as this is naive. Any time you are uncertain about whether your words are being understood or not, it is a good idea to define them.

To use words correctly you need to know precisely what they mean yourself. If you have any doubts about the meaning of words you ought to get into the habit of looking up their meaning in a reputable and up-to-date dictionary.

Dictionaries list words and phrases compiled from a survey of many sources. Unabridged dictionaries contain over five hundred thousand entries whereas the average adult knows only about ten thousand words. Be sure to check that the dictionary you are consulting is current because dictionary listings are always influx- they are constantly adding and deleting words as times change.

In addition to owning an abridged dictionary you would profit from purchasing a dictionary of synonyms. These dictionaries contain words having the same or similar meanings to the word you are looking up. Your vocabulary says a lot about you. An extensive vocabulary properly employed impresses people and creates a favorable image.

You are capable of building your vocabulary if you really want to by making a reasonable effort to do so. These tips will help you to increase your vocabulary:

* develop an attitude of intellectual inquiry (have an urge to know and grow)

* read widely on a variety of subjects or look up new words as you encounter them

* listen to what people say and analyze the context in which they used a word to figure out its meaning. It you can't determine the meaning ask the person who used it to define it for you (even presidents have been known to interrupt a speaker to ask the person to explain what a word they said meant)

* write down a new word soon after you hear it so you can remember it. Next, look up the new word. Notice how it is spelled and pronounced as well as what it means

* add the new word to your vocabulary by practicing using it frequently in sentences (both verbally and in writing)

* feel the sense of accomplishment from having expanded your vocabulary

USE THE BEST WORDS

"The important thing about any word is
how you understand it"
- Publilius Syrus

A word is a speech sound, or series of sounds, that
communicate meaning. Words are symbols that stand for
an idea, event or object. Words are not the same as the idea,
event or object themselves. Words are not the real things and
should not be confused with reality.

You have the freedom to choose what you want to say and
how you want to say it. The test for whether to use a word or
note is to ask yourself this question "Does the word fill a real
need?" If it does use it, if it doesn't don't use it.

Your constant goal should be to select just the right word
for getting your message across as clearly as possible.

Even a slight difference in words can make a tremendous
difference in their interpretation. Mark Twain once made this
perceptive observation about word differences "The difference
between the right word and the almost right word is the
difference between lightning and the lightening bug?"

There are no right words for all situations. Selecting the
exact right word to describe your thoughts and feelings is not
easy in fact it can be extremely hard. The choice is easier to

make when you possess an extensive vocabulary that allows you to pick the word which contains the fine shade of meaning that you want to convey.

This statement about language use makes an astute point "some people use language like underwear merely to cover the subject with anything while others use language like lingerie to show the subject off at its best."

Your attitude about life, people and yourself strongly influence your choice of words to use. These suggestions will assist you to make the right word choices:

* being other person rather than self-centered
* recognizing that words are only words and not reality and that they have only the meaning people give them (for eg. "sticks and stones may break my bones but words will never hurt me")
* being willing to work hard to choose only the best words to express yourself
* desiring to be candid and forthright
* wanting to use simple words and plain language
* willing to learn important information about your listeners so you can learn which words are best to use with them
* predicting the ways your words could be misunderstood so you can try to avoid using them

These tips on word use should be helpful:

* be aware that words and language are constantly changing
* know the regional differences in word use. For example, hot cakes, pancakes and Johnny cakes are all similar
* use few words rather than many words to say things
* use short words and sentences as a rule
* use simple words and familiar language
* use active instead of passive words
* say things in a positive rather than a negative way
* be explicit and precise

* use picture words. For example, brave as a lion, thundering waterfall
* state things in a concrete or tangible rather than in an abstract manner
* use gender neutral words
* choose words with an Anglo Saxon origin rather than Latin derivations
* select words that are lively and contain punch
* use specific rather than vague words and generalities
* use clear and definite words maximally and minimize the use of ambiguous words
* expect to be misunderstood at times so that you will be ready to explain and clarify what you've said

BE CAUTIONS ABOUT WORD MEANINGS

"When I use a word it means just what I choose
it to mean nothing more or less"
- Humpty Dumpty

M eaning is the sense of something that is conveyed by
language. It is that which is signified by words.
Meaning is what a speaker intends for a listener to understand
from what he/she says and it is what a listener understands from
what a speaker says to him or her.

The meaning of a word depends on the person saying it
and the person hearing it (plus the context in which the word
is used). (For example, the word holocaust has a special
meaning to a Jewish survivor of the concentration camps.) And
the word rape has a unique meaning to a rape victim. It needs
to be emphasized that a word means only what the person
saying it intends for it to mean at the certain time and under the
particular circumstances. There never has been nor ever will be
one right or God given meaning to a word.

People give similar meaning to words only to the extent
they have similar experiences. Therefore, since no two people

have ever had exactly the same experiences they cannot possibly derive exactly the same meaning for a word they say or hear.

It is helpful to view words as a map of a territory and not the actual territory itself. Like a map, words are only an approximation of what they represent.

It is impossible to predict accurately the affect a word will have in any given situation since the same word can evoke positive, neutral and negative reactions from different people. (For example the words conservative and liberal.)

It is advisable for a person speaking to constantly ask him/herself "What do I really want to say and how can I say it best?" Conversely, a person listening needs to ask him/herself "What did the speaker mean when he/she said so and so?" Both speakers and listeners need to be sensitive to the many shades and subtleties of word use. It is best not to react to a word you hear until you are sure of the speaker's intended meaning. (For example, what does a person mean who says "I'm anxious to go to the super bowl game" Is he worried or eager about going? Or, what does a woman mean when she says "Let's do lunch soon." Does she sincerely want to have lunch with the person or is she merely saying this to be polite without any intent to follow-up and have lunch together?)

Let's look at some causes of words being misunderstood:

* sloppy imprecise use of language. For example, "I need your input as soon as possible?" or "you know" or "and stuff like that"

* changing meaning of words based on the changes in the words themselves or the people speaking and listening differing experiences in life. (For example, the word gay used to mean a happy state of mind and had nothing to do with sexuality. And the word partner used to be used to describe a business relationship, whereas today it could just as easily mean co-habiting with a homosexual person. And the meaning of heart attack has a much more intense personal meaning for a person who has suffered one.) Remember meaning does not have a permanently fixed meaning)

* ambiguity caused by the multiple meaning of words. (rarely does a word have only one meaning.) For example, the word cat has dozens of meanings as does the word run. How can a person know how the speaker is using a word until the context is known? (For example, a person who is having a late supper may state "I'm starving." Compare this use of starving with a person who has just been rescued from being lost in the woods without any food for a week saying, "I'm starving." The word starving is the same but the meaning is vastly different.)

* confusion resulting from a word that is pronounced the same way but that has a different meaning. For example, saying the red book on the shelf is interesting compared with the statement, "I read the book on the shelf"

* a person's mood or feelings, at the time, influences how he/she interprets a word. For example a man may say "I hate you in anger to his wife and yet when he whispers "I hate you" in her ear during a romantic moment the word has an entirely different meaning. Or when a woman who is feeling depressed meets a friend during a walk who compliments her by saying "You certainly look nice today" may later after reflecting on this comment ask herself "I wonder what she meant by that? doesn't she think I look nice on other days?

People speaking and listening would both profit from wearing this sign continuously in their mind "Danger words at work"

STATE IDEAS CLEARLY

"I see one rule: to be clear. If I am not clear,
all my world crumbles to nothing"
- Henri Stendhal

To be clear is to be easily understood. A clear message is free of ambiguity, haziness and obscurity. Clarity creates no doubts or uncertainty. You have been clear when your listeners understand the thoughts and feelings you have expressed in essentially the same way you have intended them to be understood.

Regrettably, there is often a significant difference between what a person speaking intends to say compared to what he/she actually says and also between what he/she says and what is actually heard.

It is essential to say things clearly. You can't compromise on clarity if you want to get understood. It is the speaker's responsibility to say things clearly. Don't expect your listeners to struggle to decipher what you are really trying to tell them; they can't and won't do this. People can only react to what you say not what you intended to say.

Your goal when speaking is to have your listeners understand your words exactly as you intended them to be understood. Cicero hit the nail on the head when he stated

"The aim of speaking is not simply to be understood, but to make it impossible to be misunderstood."

You can employ a multitude of methods to be clear and thus understood:

* realize that clear expression begins with clear thinking. It is vital that you identify your purpose and keep it constantly in mind. Know exactly what you want to say and how you want to say it (always think before you speak).
* relate everything you say to your purpose
* organize your ideas in an orderly and logical sequence
* provide complete and consistent information including sufficient background material
* speak loud enough to be heard easily. Speak at a brisk pace of 120-150 words a minute. Pause at appropriate times to allow your listeners time to think about what you have said.
* pronounce your words carefully and correctly. It is best to use standard American English as your guide
* articulate your sounds carefully and properly
* give your listeners a chance to ask questions while you are speaking to secure feedback and also so that you can clarify unclear points on the spot (let people know when you begin speaking that it is okay to interrupt with questions at any time).
* adjust your speaking style and content based on the feedback you get from your listeners
* use body language to support and reinforce what you are saying
* know these important things about word use:

1. The use of words is very personal. Words have different meanings to different people in different contexts. Humpty Dumpty made this point crystal clear when he stated "When I use a word it means what I choose it to mean neither more or less"
2. Use words precisely to aid clarity. Be sure to define how you are using words especially when they have a special meaning or are highly technical

3. Use words that are familiar to your listeners as well as words that are connected to their experience. Refrain from using foreign words and unfamiliar acronyms

4. Use concrete or tangible words related to your listener's lives

5. Use specific words and phrases rather than talking in generalities

6. State things as briefly, plainly and simply as possible (and limit the amount of information you present at any one time) and use abbreviations only when they are well known

7. Cite relevant examples and tell stories to help explain complicated ideas. Comparisons and contrasts are also helpful when explaining complex and unfamiliar information

8. Develop an extensive vocabulary so you can select the best and most precise word to use to make a point more clearly

9. Use correct English. Be sure to have your tenses agree.

Be certain to make your antecedents obvious when you use pronouns. In addition, have your subjects and verbs agree in form.

* Repeat important points several times to reinforce them. For example, tell people what you are going to tell them, tell them and then tell them what you have told them

* Make clear transitions to help people know when you are leaving one point and proceeding to the next one (numbering your points is an effective way to show transitions)

*Help your listeners to visualize the objects or events you are talking about by using lively and picturesque language that conjures up word pictures (eg. little red school house) Visual aids also create mental images to support your words

* Appeal to both sides of your listener's brain. Appeal to the left side to have them apply logic, sequence and order to what you are saying and appeal to the right side of the in brain to help them see the total picture and the spatial or artistic dimensions of your presentation

* avoid frequent use of these confusing kinds of words and phrases because they disguise what you really mean or because they overly soften what you really intend to convey:

1. euphemisms-for example, saying pleasingly plump for fat, passed on for died, misspoke for lied etc.

2. politically correct-for example, love child for bastard, disadvantaged for poor and physically challenged for physically handicapped.

3. double speak-for example, open secret, deliberate speed, bitter sweet, negative growth, working vacation

SPEAK CORRECT GRAMMAR

"The first thing you should attend to is to speak in its
greatest purity and according to the rules of grammar;
for we must never offend against grammar"
- Lord Chesterfield

Grammar is a system of rules for the use of language. It is
the study of the classes of words, their inflections, their
functions and relationships in a sentence. A speaker who uses
correct grammar follows the principles or rules of word use.

Grammatical rules provide the foundation for communication.
Effective communication requires the correct use of grammar.
Fortunately, the proper use of grammar can be learned and the
improper use of grammar corrected.

It is important that you constantly check your grammar for
correctness, for as Confucius aptly put it

"If language is not correct,
then what is said is not meant.
if what is said is not meant,
then what ought to be done remains undone"

A speaker's errors in grammar and pronunciation are immediately apparent to his/her listeners. These mistakes affect the speaker's credibility.

When a speaker makes a grammatical faux pas it is obvious to his listeners and they are inclined to pay more attention to the mistakes than to what is being said. Consequently, their understanding suffers.

Here are several common problems of grammar that interfere with a speaker getting understood:

* incorrect word choice-for example, use of went instead of gone and seen rather than saw
* confusion resulting from improper use of nouns and pronouns
* disagreement of subject and verb (for example, they was)
* missed tenses (for example, past and present in the same sentence)
* careless use of modifiers (adjectives and adverbs)
* use of double negatives (for example, I'm not going there no more)
* unnecessary redundancies (for example, killed dead)
* poor sentence structure

A sentence is a group of words that express a complete thought. It is best to limit a sentence to one thought. It is wise to speak in short sentences to enhance understanding.

All parts of a sentence should agree (be consistent) with all other parts of the sentence. This means that:

1. each verb agrees with its subject
2. each pronoun agrees with its antecedent (noun)
3. all tenses agree

Active sentences, in which the subject carries out the action of the verb, are preferable to passive sentences because active sentences are more forceful and interesting (for example, active-baseball fans favor high scoring games and passive high scoring games are favored by fans)

Let's examine how you can use five of the seven parts of speech in a way that increases your listener's comprehension. The parts of speech include: nouns, pronouns, verbs, adverbs, adjectives, prepositions and conjunctions.

1. nouns-Nouns name a person, place, things, thoughts and feelings. Nouns are used as the subject of a sentence. To promote clarity use only one noun at a time rather than stringing two or more together. A single noun as a subject should have a corresponding single pronoun. (For example, Joan she and Jane and Helen they. Also, the gender of a noun and pronoun should agree Sharon-she)

2. pronouns-Pronouns are words that take the place of nouns. The subject for which a pronoun is substituted is called its antecedent. Every pronoun should refer clearly to its antecedent because ambiguous pronouns confuse the people listening. To aid clarify a pronoun should be placed close to its antecedent noun because an additional noun standing between the first noun and its pronoun may confuse listeners

There are two cases (classes) of pronouns (1) the nominative and (2) the objective. Nominative pronouns include the words: I, we, he, she, it and they.

The objective pronouns are: us, you, him, her, it and them.

3. verbs-A verb expresses action or describes a condition. It acts as the quarterback in the sentence by directing the play or by conveying additional information. Verbs can be the strongest or weakest words in a sentence.

There are two kinds of verbs (1) active and (2) passive. Active verbs express action that is performed by the subject of a sentence. On the other hand, passive verbs express action that is received by or performed upon the subject of a sentence.

It is best to use strong and active verbs whenever possible because they convey a more definite sense of movement and are more lively than are passive verbs.

Make sure the number of subjects and verbs agree. For example, salaries have been rising instead of salaries has been rising.

Also use the correct form of a verb. For example, she has gone to the movies instead of she has went to the movies.

4. adverbs-Adverbs are modifiers that describe verbs, adjectives and other adverbs. They specify in what manner, when, where, and how much. It is a good idea to limit the use of adverbs as much as possible because they are normally superfluous. (For example, he clenched his teeth tightly.)

5. adjectives-Adjectives are words describing nouns. They specify things such as sizes, color and number (they modify nouns). It is wise to restrict the use of adjectives as much as possible since they are generally unnecessary (For example, the large giant.)

We should take a brief look at tenses. There are three kinds of tenses: (1) past, (2) present and (3) future. Here is an example of each:

past-he went to the store yesterday
present-he is going to the store right now
future-he will be going to the store tomorrow

It is best to speak primarily in the present tense because it elicits the most interest from the people listening.

USE SIMPLE WORDS

"Simplify, simplify, simplify" Henry David Thoreau

Saying something simply is saying it by using plain words and uncomplicated language. Simple speaking avoids the use of fancy words, pinpoints the key ideas and gets straight to the heart of the matter.

There is real power in speaking simply. Important ideas do not have to be expressed in a complicated manner. People who really know what they are talking about can say things clearly and simply. They use words only to express themselves rather than to impress people (truly big people use little words).

If there are several ways of saying the same thing elect to say it in the simplest way. It needs to be emphasized that use of simple language doesn't reflect a simple mind. And simplicity does not mean that your language must be simplistic and sound as though you are talking down to people.

Two other points need to be stressed:

1. Use of overly simple language can insult and turn off your listeners

2. Big words are not always objectionable. They are okay if the subject requires their use (For example, something highly

technical.) They are also alright to use if they sound natural for the speaker and are appropriate for the particular listeners.

These suggestions will assist you to speak simply:

* use short words, short sentences, and short paragraphs (beware of using four and five syllable words).
* adapt your language to your listeners-use words only if they are suitable for your listeners
* use concrete and tangible words as much as you can (avoid abstractions as much as possible)
* define all important words and phrases that are not crystal clear
* avoid using foreign words and phrases
* refrain from employing specialized and technical terms, jargon, slang and colloquialisms
* speak concisely-cut out any unnecessary words
* limit the amount of information you share at any one time, especially if it is new and complicated

The following quotations speak plainly, powerfully and succinctly about the beauty of simplicity:

1. Henry Wadsworth Longfellow
"In character, manner in all things the supreme excellence is simplicity"

2. Abraham Lincoln
"Speak so the most lowly can understand and the rest will have no difficulty"

3. Ralph Waldo Emerson
"An orator or writer is never successful until he has learned to make his words smaller than his ideas"

A speaker would be well advised to keep these quotations in mind when choosing the best way to say things to people.

USE PRECISE WORDS

"When you say something, make sure you have said it"
- William Strunk and E.B. White

To state something precisely is to do it exactly. It is to define it sharply and minutely.

The precise meaning of words is influenced by the speaker's and listener's backgrounds, experiences and emotional state at the time. Also, the more abstract the word the more varied its interpretation.

Here are a few examples of abstract words that invite multiple interpretation of their meanings: freedom, justice, patriotism, truth, honesty, soon, large, and beautiful.

The more precisely you can word your message the better you will be understood. Therefore, your goal should be to express yourself as exactly as possible. You want to leave no doubts in your listeners mind as to what your comments mean.

Unfortunately, regardless of how precise you words are there will be some difficulty in getting what you have said interpreted correctly. This uncertainty exists because of the differences in people, the nuances of language, and the fact that words are always only an approximation of the things and events they are describing (much like a map is only an approximation of the actual territory it represents).

Imprecise wording results from fuzzy thinking, saying the first word that pops into your mind and the speaker's limited vocabulary.

The first step in stating something precisely is clear thinking about what you want to say. Next, you need to select the words that most accurately express the exact shade of meaning for what you want to convey and have your listener hear.

You can improve your use of just the right word to get your message across by:

* enlarging your vocabulary
* looking up various synonyms that you can use and choosing the best one
* using words that create mental images or pictures in peoples' minds of the person, thing or event being talked about (For example, the little red school house or the plain white church with the tall steeple on the village green).
* thinking through exactly what you want to say before saying anything
* knowing your listeners backgrounds and experiences with the subject

Here are several examples that emphasizes the differences between precise (P) and imprecise wording (I):

* I - I need the report as soon as possible

   P - I need the weekly production report by noon today
* I - I will be out of the office for several days next week

   P - I will be in Tucson on Tuesday next week and will return to the office by one o'clock on Wednesday
* I - While you are at the market be sure to get something for lunches as well as some fish and dessert

   P - When you go to Safeway be sure to get 1 pound of provolone cheese and 2 pounds of hamburger, for lunches as well as two one pound salmon steaks and a Pepperidge Farm coconut cake

USE SPECIFIC WORDS

"Be as specific as you possibly can when
talking with people"
- anonymous

B eing specific is limiting or restricting what you are saying
to a particular person, thing or event. It is the opposite of
being general or vague.

The more general and the less specific a word or phrase is
the more difficult it is to understand. Words work best when
they convey specific meaning and worse when they are loaded
with generalizations and ambiguities. By being specific you
promote understanding and take much of the guesswork out
of what you are saying. On the other hand, when you speak in
generalities and vaguely you cause confusion and create
misunderstanding.

You can make your statements more specific and concrete
if you do these things:

* select you words carefully. Don't be content to settle for
the first words that pop into your head
* use precise wording that conveys the exact information
you want to share

* prefer language that is specific rather than general, concrete rather than vague, and tangible instead of abstract
* say words that create mental images or pictures in your listener's mind
* refer to actual people, places and events
* cite the names of people rather than using the pronouns: he, she and they
* give definite times and dates instead of approximations
* provide all the relevant facts and details without being excessive
* state statistics and actual events to pin things down
* use several relevant examples and anecdotes

Now, let's look at a few examples that contrast general (g) with specific (s) wording when communicating:

1. G - The child enjoys her soft toy.
    S - The two year old enjoys playing with her soft teddy bear.
2. G - The father and son went to the ballgame in the spring
    S - The father and his son Bill went to see a Dodger baseball game on the night of April 10th.
3. G - I need you to give this report a top priority.
    S - I need you to get me the monthly financial report by noon tomorrow.
4. G - I need the project completed as soon as possible,.
    S - I need the Canfield project on my desk no later than nine AM next Monday November 1st.
5. G - Your monthly report was unsatisfactory and probably needs to be revised.
    S - Section four of your monthly report needs to be more detailed before I can okay it.

BE EXPLICIT

"The more explicit you can be the better"
- Walter St. John

You are being explicit when your statements fully reveal what you are thinking. It involves saying something without being vague or ambiguous. Things are stated rather than merely implied. An explicit statement leaves no doubts about your meaning or intent.

It is wise to be as explicit as possible when you speak to assist your listeners comprehension. And conversely, it is best to avoid being implicit (you are being implicit when the essence of what you are talking about is not actually stated or revealed).

It is interesting to note that some cultures, such as the Japanese, believe that many ideas are best communicated without being explicit. They prefer that meaning be derived intuitively. However generally the more explicit you can be the better. It is unwise to require your listeners to guess at the true meaning of what you are saying.

Here are a couple of examples of explicit statements:

1. The president has had a severe heart attack and will be in intensive care ward at Sacred Hearts Hospital for the next week according to his personal physician Dr. Jonathan Morse.

2. The Smiths paid cash for a two million dollar home with twenty rooms. The brick hundred year old home is located on the beach 2 miles north of Kennebunkport, Maine.

You can speak explicitly by:

* being as precise as possible
* providing examples and explanations
* being specific and avoiding being general
* disclosing fully and honestly exactly what is on your mind

USE FAMILIAR WORDS

"Every new movement or manifestation of human
activity when unfamiliar in peoples' minds is sure to
be misrepresented and misunderstood"
- Edward Carpenter

F amiliar words and language are marked by informality.
They are easily recognized by people. Familiar words are
frequently said, heard and experienced.

Your goal when speaking is to make your meaning instantly
understandable. Don't force your listeners to exert a lot of effort
to figure out what you are saying. It doesn't make sense to use
words your listeners don't know. Remember, your purpose in
communicating is to express not impress (people who really
know a subject are able to use simple and plain words when
talking about it).

Common sense dictates that you increase the possibility of
being misunderstood when you use unfamiliar words and
language. Also note that a word that is familiar to one person
may not be familiar to other people. The sage Hippocrates once
perceptively stated "Nothing detracts from the clarity of
language as much as the use of unfamiliar words".

Here are some tips on how to use familiar words and language that will help you to get understood:

* use everyday words and phrases that people know and are comfortable with
* let short familiar words convey how you think and feel about things
* show how your new ideas relate to already known and familiar ideas
* use technical and specialized terms cautiously
* provide testimony and quotations from people your listeners know and respect
* cite examples associated with your listeners backgrounds and experiences
* refrain from using foreign words, slang, clichés or worn out expressions such as

pretty as a picture	can't see the woods from the trees
the writing is on the wall	take to the woodshed
slow as molasses	chip off the old block
right as rain	sharp as a tack

Now let's examine how much clearer the meaning is with simple familiar words contrasted with longer and unfamiliar words:

familiar	unfamiliar	familiar	unfamiliar
learned	erudite	enemy	protagonist
unnecessary	superfluous	extra	extraneous
neat	fastidious	aware	cognizant
small	diminutive	large	gargantuan
talkative	loquacious	excitable	exuberant
boundaries	parameters	generous	magnanimous
count	enumerate	benefactor	philanthropist
hungry	famished	sad	morose

This final thought from Corinthians emphasizes the importance of saying things plainly and in familiar terms:

"Except ye utter by tongues
easy to be understood
how shall it be known what is spoken
for ye shall speak into the air"

USE GENDER NEUTRAL WORDS

"The differences in focus on messages and meta
messages can give man and women different points
of view on almost any comment."
- Dorothy Tannen

Gender refers to a person's sex-male or female. Gender neutral words lack bias and prejudice, they don't favor one sex more than the other.

Words can make a difference! They can create positive or negative attitudes and feelings about people, things and events. Historically the English language has been male oriented, favored men and been biased against women. Gender neutral language treats men and women fairly and as equals, whereas sexist language is biased against women.

The frequent, even if inadvertent, use of sexist language can create relational problems, interfere with understanding, and even cause resentment.

A speaker needs to acknowledge the existence of sexist language and identify which words are sexist so he/she can avoid using them. He/she also needs to know how to use gender neutral language so that they can build bridges rather than create barriers to understanding.

There is no denying that men and women communicate differently. They have differing communications attitudes, perspectives and styles.

Men and women could both benefit from learning how each other communicates. Knowing the similarities and differences could reduce misunderstanding.

Recognizing that gender biased language can upset people and lead to misunderstanding, your goal should be to become aware of what constitutes sexist language and to use gender neutral (fair) words routinely.

Here is a partial list of contrasting gender neutral words with sexist words. There are many more gender related words but these examples should suffice to make the point adequately:

gender neutral	gender biased	gender neutral	gender biased
flight attendant	stewardess	fire fighter	fireman
mail carrier	mailman	police officer	policeman
human kind	mankind	staffing	manning
sales rep	salesman	chairperson	chairman
engineer	lady engineer	woman	girl
executive	manager	womens' college	girls' school
Miss Jones	honey	my secretary	my girl
nice appearance	sexy appearance	Mrs. Jones	Betty

Now, let's take a look at some important differences that are generally present in most male-female communication that you should be aware of in order to improve your communication with the opposite sex.

* women talk on a more personal and emotional level whereas men emphasize facts and play down emotion
* men tend to make statements and lecture whereas women tend to listen and ask questions
* men tend to get right to the point and focus on solving problems while women are more process and details oriented
* men typically don't listen as well and interrupt frequently. Women listen better, interrupt less often or differently (For expmple, by giving feedback)

* men usually speak more directly or authoritatively and give orders. Conversely, women make suggestions, are more indirect and less assertive

* men are commonly more competitive, disagree more often and are more comfortable stating their opinions and arguing. However, women are more cooperative, more reluctant to disagree or to argue

* men are concerned with maintaining their status in conversations while women are more interested in connecting with others

* women tend to sit opposite each other and to look directly at each other whereas men sit at an angle and look at each other indirectly

* women tend to talk with some hesitation and a rising inflection in their voices which suggests tentativeness and uncertainty to the men listening

* women are inclined to be more compassionate and politically correct when talking than are men

* men usually talk in generalities and abstractions whereas women stress tangibles and specifics (for example, women refer to their personal experiences more often than do men.)

* women who engage in small talk and to chit-chat while men are usually uncomfortable with and avoid this kind of talk

Please note much of this information is from Dorothy Tannen's books on male-female communication. If you are especially interested in male-female communication you may want to read Dorothy Tannen's excellent books on this subject.

BE AWARE OF WORDS THAT QUALIFY MEANING

"Stating qualifiers with unnecessary auxiliaries or conditions sound irresolute. Make definite assertions. Avoid tame, colorless, hesitating non-commital language - William Strunk and E.B. White

Qualifying words are used to moderate and limit the meaning of something said. They are commonly used to make statements sound less harsh, offensive or intimidating.

Your goal when speaking should be to say what you mean and to mean what you say. Conversely, qualifying words and statements interfere with your achieving clear understanding of what you are saying. Qualifiers are often used to provide a hedge or escape from what is being said. For example, politicians and bureaucrats frequently are guilty of using qualifying words to protect or avoid committing themselves (for eg. the weasel words maybe and perhaps).

By using qualifying words inappropriately you diminish your credibility and image as a straightforward, honest person with integrity. You risk making everything you say becoming suspect. Therefore, it is advisable to use as few qualifying words as possible when describing what you think and feel about a matter.

To be fair, it is important to recognize that qualifying your statements when you truly lack information or are uncertain about something is acceptable if not advisable. (For example here are some statements that are appropriate in these circumstances:)

* "my best guess is"
* "I really don't know but I would imagine…"
* "I agree in principle, but need to know the details before I can …"
* " I really can't answer that because I simply don't have enough information to even speculate"

Here are several examples of qualifying words and statements that you should not use:

* "I'll try" (this avoids accepting responsibility for getting something done)
* "I forgot" (also avoids taking responsibility for failing to do something that should have been done)
* "I can't" (this is a lie if you really can do it but don't want to)
* "I'll do it when I can get around to it" (this expresses vagueness and is without a sincere intent to do something)
* "well yes and no" (avoids taking a stand and giving a definite answer)
* "I think that is generally true" (what about this time?)
* "I think we should proceed with deliberate speed" (how fast or slow is this?)
* "I view that with cautious optimism" (nothing is really said here)
* "This is only my own opinion so don't quote me…" (lacks conviction)

USE TECHNICAL WORDS
CAUTIOUSLY

"A word whose meaning is perfectly clear to one person
may be totally misunderstood by someone else"
- anonymous

Technical language has a special and unusual meaning and use. It is designed or fitted for one particular purpose, use or occupation. It pertains to a specialized field of knowledge such as science. Technical language is specialized with limited application.

Each science, technology and occupation has developed its own distinct language to use to achieve an exactness or preciseness of expression that promotes understanding and discourages multiple meanings.

Technical language promotes understanding by specialists in the same field but can't be readily understood by the average person.

Despite the communications barriers it creates, there is a proper place for specialized language and jargon. In many instances it is best for people in technical fields to employ highly specialized language because it offers a precision of meaning that might be lacking otherwise. When discussing especially significant matters it is advisable to read technical subjects content word for word to minimize the possibility of it being misunderstood (and for the record).

Try to use plain words and simple language whenever possible. And do your best to avoid using technical or specialized language with non-specialists.

Fortunately, there are some counter measures you can take to overcome problems caused by the use of technical language. These measures include:

* Having ready access to and consulting an up-to-date dictionary promptly when needed
* Identifying, in advance, the technical words and specialized language that you intend to use that is new or unfamiliar to your listeners
* Defining unfamiliar technical terms at the beginning of your presentation
* Stating things simply and briefly (use familiar language)
* Refraining from using acronyms and abbreviations especially if they are not commonly known
* Avoiding using slang, colloquialisms and foreign words
* Watching for and being alert to cues that indicate that your listeners are confused by what you are saying (e.g., facial expressions and body language)
* Stopping immediately when your listeners appear lost and ask for their questions or furnish additional information
* Providing examples familiar to your listeners to make your point in a more concrete fashion

Language is always in a state of flux. New words are constantly being introduced to the English language. Also, the meaning of existing words is continuously changing.

New words are usually associated with a new event, activity or vocation. These examples of the new terms being used should illustrate this point.

* Communications field: fax, E-mail, the internet, Kindle and Skype
* Computer field: texting, web-site, Facebook, blog

* Space industry: lift off, all systems go, mission scrubbed
* Transportation field: jet lag and ground positioning system
* Medicine: body mass index, and new labels and diseases e.g., Alzheimer's and autism
* Social activities: chill out, rapping, hang out and hooking up
* Descriptions of people: spaced out, druggie, love child, and wicked awesome

In addition to new words being misunderstood, further confusion results from the changing meaning of existing words. Here are several examples of common existing words whose meaning has changed drastically:

* gay from happy to male homo-sexual
* partner from business associate to same sex living together
* cool from low temperature to impressive or good
* challenged from questioned or disputed to handicapped

In addition to single words many new phrases are being used such as:

* throw under the bus
* on the same page
* at the end of the day

The list of specialized words, new words and words with a changed meaning is endless.

AVOID USING PROBLEM WORDS

"But words once spoken can never be recalled"
- Wentworth Dillon

A speaker who avoids certain words refrains from using them. She doesn't use negative or objectionable words that evoke an unfavorable reaction from the people listening. Words can create three kinds of reactions (1) positive, (2) neutral, (3) negative. Your goal is to select the words that will result in positive responses and at the worst neutral reactions. In order to get understood better conscientiously avoid using any words or phrases that will receive unfavorable reactions.

There are many types of words that you are well advised to avoid. These include:

* gender biased such as fireman or firefighter and postman for postal carrier
* showy, fancy and pretentious words such as erudite for learned, utilize for use and philanthropic for humanitarian
* vague, general, and imprecise words such as: bring me several nails, be home early, drive faster, or I need it as soon as possible
* overused worn out words that have lost their impact (sometimes called clichés or trite) such as: slow as molasses,

black of night, crack of dawn, pig in a poke, old as the hills and it doesn't take a rocket scientist to....

* empty, meaningless words that don't say anything. For example, you know, bright future ahead of him, whatever, and kill dead

* condescending and insulting words that imply superiority such as: dumb as dirt, stupid, idiot, and white trash

* wishy-washy, qualifying words that are self-protective and evasive such as: perhaps, usually, maybe, kind of tired and somewhat excited

* hard to pronounce words that have acceptable alternatives. For example: numbers for statistics

* loaded slanted and stacked words and phrases such as: I'm sure you agree with me that or don't you think that we should...

* excessive euphemisms that weaken or disguise the point you are making. For example: passed away for died, revenue enhancement for taxes and obese for fat

* politically correct phrases that water down or weaken what you're saying such as: physically challenged for handicapped, Asian for Oriental, resigned for fired

* vulgar and offensive words including the various four letter words, tramp, queer, pissed off and pervert

* negatively stated phrases such as: don't forget to, not bad, things have been worse

* emotionally charged, inflammatory, red flag words that elicit powerful emotions and distract listeners such as: welfare, radical, addict, union, management, red neck, womanizer

* slang, colloquialisms and regional words. For example, you are in high cotton when things are good, throw under the bus, right as rain, crazy as a loon and cut off the lights

* foreign words, especially those with Latin routes. For example: que sera sera, muy pronto, adios, and manana

* jargon, technical language and buzz words used in certain specialized fields such as medicine, law, science and engineering

* use of acronyms unfamiliar to most people. These include:

SOP for standard operating procedure
SWAG for scientific wild assed guess

ASAP for as soon as possible
TGIF for thank God it's Friday
24-7 for twenty-four hours seven days a week

SECTION 6
CLARIFY THE MESSAGE

THINK BEFORE YOU SPEAK

"It is necessary to think before speaking, but you
must also think while speaking"
- Kenneth McFarland

When people think they reflect or ponder on something. They consider and exercise judgment about a matter.

Every communication begins with a thought. Clear thinking is the starting point for clear speaking. You can't expect something that is fuzzy and unclear in your own mind to be clear and coherent to the people listening to you.

It is essential that you think about what you want to say and how you want to say it before you say anything important. By taking a little time to think over what you want to say initially, you may save substantial time later when you need to correct something ill advised that you said because you said it off the top of your head.

A thoughtless comment is rarely effective and may prove to be disastrous. Remember, once you have uttered words you can't recall them (people may forgive something you said in haste that was offensive but they never forget being offended).

Before saying anything important it is a good idea to pause and ask yourself four questions:

1. What exactly do I want to say?
2. Why do I need to say it?
3. How can I say it most clearly and tactfully?
4. What will the listeners' reactions probably be?

The quality of your thinking depends on the quality of the information you have on the matter. The ideas you express can't be any better than the information you have available for forming your thoughts.

When you need to make an important presentation before a group you would be well advised to:

* think about the topic for several days. During this time mull over different ideas and information that you would like to convey without making any decision about them at that time

* determine your specific purpose and write it down in a brief statement

* jot down your ideas on the topic freely as they come to mind without considering their importance, order and relevance

* research the topic to gather the best information from objective and reputable sources

* analyze the data collected. Keep only the most impressive information and discard the rest

* develop your outline listing your main points in a logical sequence to guide your thinking (see the organization section of this book for details re: organization)

* determine the essential information and details you want to include to support your main points

* think about your listeners. What are their expectations, attitudes and understanding of your subject?

* think about the key ideas you want to share and how to best word them

* consider the probable questions you will be asked by your listeners

* look up the proper pronunciation of any unfamiliar words you plan to say so you will know the right way to pronounce them

* put away your outline and notes for several days without thinking about them

* look over your outline and related information with a fresh outlook

* finalize your preparation

* think about the place you will be delivering your talk (see the setting section of this book for details)

* pause to think over your listeners' questions before answering them (it helps to repeat the questions aloud to make sure you understand them before responding)

* This quotation by Pericles is worth remembering in this context "The man who can think and does not know how to express what he thinks is at the level of him who cannot think."

DEFINE WORDS

"Define it well" Alfred Tennyson

A definition explains the essential meaning of words. It establishes boundary lines or determines the limits of meaning. Definitions attempt to create a common ground for communicating among different people especially if they have widely divergent backgrounds.

No word means the same thing to any two people because the meaning of words is an intensely personal matter. Meaning exists only within a person and is always contextual. Humpty Dumpty made this point crystal clear when he said to Alice "When I use a word it means what I want it to mean, neither more or less."

It is especially important to define words precisely when they possess several possible meanings or are technical in nature. For example, the words cat and run have dozens of possible meanings.

Your goal when speaking is to use words that are as specific, clear and familiar as possible.

It is helpful to get into the habit of consulting a dictionary whenever you want to pick the best word that says exactly what you want to say.

When using a dictionary remember that a dictionary has limitations. It only provides the general or usual meaning of a word at the time the dictionary was published.

The words listed in a dictionary are constantly changing to reflect current word use. Also, over time the meaning of certain words change. For example, the current versus the previous meaning of such words as gay, partner and liberal.

You can improve your ability to define words and expand your vocabulary by:

* having ready access to a current and reputable dictionary (preferably access to a book of synonyms also)

* defining all technical and specialized terms as well as words that are new or unfamiliar to your listeners (when in doubt as to whether your listeners understand a word be sure to define it)

* offering synonyms when saying an unfamiliar word

* explaining what a word is not or something that a word does not mean. For example, "by co-existence with Russia I don't mean appeasement" or by compromise I don't mean capitulating or surrendering on key principles

* being careful not to talk down to people when defining a word or phrase

BE BRIEF

"Prune thou thy words" Cardinal Newman

To be brief is to be concise and of short duration. It is using few words and short sentences when saying something.

Your goal when speaking is to find the simplest, shortest and most direct way to say something and yet to include all the necessary information. Your objectives should be to find the right balance between being concise and complete. It is a mistake to omit essential information just to be brief.

Your listeners appreciate it when you are brief. They can pay better attention and retain what you have said easier and longer when you are concise. Also, your main ideas stand out when you limit their number.

An important part of being brief is knowing what not to say. And once you have decided on what to include in your message it is essential that you know when it is time to stop talking.

There are many ways you can be brief and thus enhance your chances of getting understood. Here are several of the best ones:

* know your purpose and keep it constantly in mind
* limit information presented at one time avoid overkill

* include only relevant and essential information
* cut out all unnecessary background and details
* eliminate all information already known or obvious to your listeners
* get directly to the point and stick to it-don't ramble
* use repetition only when it has a definite purpose
* use short words and sentences without being terse
* refrain from using non-essential modifiers e.g. adjectives and adverbs
* stop immediately after saying what needs to be said
* cut out filler words that say nothing and waste time e.g. uh, er, um, you know and like
* make every word count,. Get rid of empty words such as these that say nothing: you know, and stuff like that, whatever, and okay at the end of sentences
* question the need for every word when in doubt leave it out

Omit a phrase when one word will suffice. For example:

because instead of due to the fact
if instead of in the event that
remember instead of don't forget
soon instead of in due course
although instead of in spite of the fact
please instead of we would ask that

Brief messages are often more powerful than long ones because the crux of the message doesn't get lost in a sea of words. The list of such powerful words is endless. Here are several examples of the most powerful ones:

* the Lord's prayer 71 words
* the Ten Commandments 297 words
* the Gettysburg Address 271 words
* marriage vows I do 2 words
* give me liberty or give me death 7 words
* I love you 3 words

EMPHASIZE IMPORTANT INFORMATION

"Failure to emphasize any words or the wrong
words robs your message of meaning"
- John Irwin and Marjorie Rosenberger-

Y ou emphasize something when you stress it or give it
special importance. Stress is frequently used as a synonym
for emphasis.

Certain information is more important than other
information in any message. It is essential that you get your
main points and central ideas clear in your own mind before
sharing them with your listeners (you can't make clear to other
people what isn't clear to yourself).

Unless you emphasizes which information is the most
important, your listeners will tend to view all the information
as equally important. To improve your chances of getting your
key points understood you need to identify them for your
listeners.

Fortunately, there are a number of excellent ways that you
can use to stress your main points:

* give important information more time than the less
important

* position your most important words and sentences at the beginning and ending of your comments (people remember what you say best at the start and finish of your talk)

* limit the number of words re: your main points so that they will not get lost in the midst of trivial details

* change your voice volume, vary your pitch level and tone of voice to stress something

* vary your rate of speaking. For example, talk more slowly when stating your main points

* pause to give your important ideas time to be absorbed

* use compatible facial expressions, body movement and gestures to support your words

* reinforce crucial data by presenting it in more than one way. For example, compare and contrast, using visuals or catchy words and memorable phrases

* cite relevant quotations and statistics pertaining to your main points to add punch

* ask rhetorical questions after saying something important. For example, "now why is what I've said so important to your future?"

* tell relevant anecdotes and stories that create greater interest

* cite examples and give complete explanations

* enumerate key points. For example 1, 2, 3, 4 or A.B.C.D

* repeat and restate major ideas with the same or different words and phrases to reinforce them in your listeners minds

* offer periodic summaries of the main points especially at the end of your presentation

* use picture words and visuals to accompany your words to pound important points home

* draw attention to your main points by saying things such as:

1. "pay close attention to this point because…."
2. "Be sure to remember this…."
3. "Let me repeat this crucial point…."
4. "Now what I am about to say is the essence of my presentation so listen carefully"

MAKE DEFINITE TRANSITIONS

"Tell them what you're going to tell them tell
them and tell them what you've told them"
- anonymous

A transition is the passing from one subject to the next
subject while speaking. Transitions are words and phrases
that indicate when a speaker has completed one idea or point
and is moving on to the next idea or point.

Transitions are necessary for you to get understood; their
primary function is to alert the person listening that a new idea
is being introduced. They are also used to hold a listeners
interest. When you neglect to use proper transitions you make
it difficult for your listeners to follow the sequence of your
thoughts.

Make your transitions as simple and smooth as possible
(avoid abrupt or sudden transitions).

You may indicate transitions by:

* changing your voice tone or inflections
* pausing between topics
* gesturing and moving of the body in a noticeable and
meaningful manner (eg. turning your head or body)

* telling your listeners that you are moving to the next point

There are many words that you can say to show transitions. These include:

furthermore	moreover	lastly
next	instead	but
in addition	meanwhile	conversely
consequently	again	similarly
therefore	finally	subsequently

There are also a number of phrases that you can use to indicate transitions:

* on the other hand
* to sum this up
* now, let's turn to my next point
* this brings me to my fourth point
* so much for the present now let's examine the future
* we have listed the causes now let's look at possible solutions
* in conclusion....

USE REPETITION PROPERLY

"And oft repeated, they believe em" Matthew Prior

R epetition is the act of repeating. It is doing or saying something over, again, or several times.

There are two kinds of appropriate repetition:

1. Verbatim

Verbatim is the repeating of a word or phrase using exactly the same words a second time.

2. Paraphrasing

Paraphrasing is the repeating of the same idea or information a second time, but by using different words or phrases.

There are four legitimate purposes for repeating something:

* to clarify what was said
* to emphasizes key information
* to give your listeners time to digest what was said
* to provide your listeners a second chance to hear what you've just finished saying in the event they were distracted by something while you were talking (For example, a loud noise).

You should repeat words and phrases only when it serves a definite purpose. Useless repetition may bore your listeners and cause them to tune you out if it occurs frequently. Also, if you repeat something without a reason you may appear disorganized to your listeners.

Here is an example of a verbatim repetition contrasted with a paraphrased repetition.

1. Verbatim-is the repeating of a word or phrase using exactly the same words a second time.

The Boston Red Sox welcomed the left handed pitcher with great enthusiasm.

The Boston Red Sox welcomed the left handed pitcher with great enthusiasm.

2. Paraphrase-The Boston Red Sox organization greeted their newly acquired southpaw hurler to the pitching staff with unrestrained exuberance.

OFFER APPROPRIATE EXPLANATIONS

"I wish he would explain his explanation"
- Samuel Johnson

To explain is to make known and understandable. It is to make something not immediately obvious comprehensible.

It is a good idea to explain anything that is new or complicated. You can't simply rely on a general statement and hope to be understood.

There are several things you can do to explain something to your listeners:

* sharing experiences or doing something together that are related to the information you are trying to get across
* reviewing step by step a difficult procedure or process (for example, assembling something or demonstrating how to do something such as giving 1st aid or how to drive a car)
* describing the details of something (for example, route for a trip)
* telling a story involving the ideas you are offering
* role playing a technique. (For example, holding a counseling session or how to manage conflict)

* using the case study approach that includes all the factors to consider when solving a problem
* listing the ingredients for making something (for example, baking an apple pie)
* drawing a diagram or a map to visually depict what you are saying
* using a visual aid to present a mental image or something.
* providing examples to make a generality or abstraction more clear, specific and tangible

Here are several examples that demonstrate how the use of examples can make a general point more clear and meaningful:

1. There are an increasing number of people who are chronically ill. The number is rising because of: an aging population, rapid changes in life cycle, pollution, peoples' obesity and lack of exercise.

2. College costs are excessive and constantly rising (for example, tuition is sky high, books cost hundreds of dollars, food and dorm costs are rising and expensive loans are increasingly required).

3. People are reluctant to run for public offices because of the pressure and expenses involved. These include: excessive time demands, interruptions to family routines, personal attacks by the media, campaigning expenses, and the bitter political climate.

PROVIDE FREQUENT EXAMPLES

"Example is the school of mankind" Edmund Burke

An example is a brief reference to specific items or events. Examples clarify, reinforce and personalize ideas. An example uses a specific case or instance to explain a general statement. Examples provide additional details.

You use examples to clarify or provide more information about something. By using examples you can minimize multiple interpretations of what you have said.

When using examples it is wise to employ real life rather than hypothetical examples because most people understand these better. The best examples are those that are familiar to and match the experiences of your listeners.

Strive to support every new or complex idea with at least one example. This helps comprehension because examples often create word pictures for your listeners. Word pictures make generalities and abstractions more specific and concrete and therefore more easily understood.

Here are a few examples of how you can make generalities and abstractions clearer and easier to grasp: (notice how each clarifies the main point stated)

1. Many churches are in financial trouble and suffering because of this. (e.g. more and more churches are closing,

encountering staffing difficulties and suffering from lower attendance)

2. Feelings of patriotism are bolstered by symbols and rituals (e.g. the statue of liberty, the Washington Monument, citing the pledge of allegiance and the singing of the national anthem).

3. People are increasing upset with their medical care (e.g. the cost is ever increasing, there are long waits to see doctors, appointments are rushed and insurance costs are high).

4. Democracies are superior to dictatorship (e.g. there is more freedom of expression and movement, greater economic opportunity, fair trials, free elections and less police brutality).

5. Recessions really harm people (e.g. people lose their homes, marital friction is created, people are depressed and many people lose hope).

Remember, the best examples are those that relate directly to the life experiences of the people listening to you.

SUMMARIZE KEY POINTS

"To summarize is a wise thing" anonymous

You summarize a presentation when you review the main points stated in a succinct fashion. It is to sum up all that has been said that is especially noteworthy. Synonyms for summarizing are: an abridgement, an abstract or a synopsis.

Summaries are used as signposts to assist your listeners to see the overall picture of your presentation (by pulling all of the main points together).

There are three kinds of summaries you can use: (1) preliminary, (2) periodic and (3) final.

A preliminary summary occurs at the beginning of a presentation to provide an overview of the main points you are going to make in your talk.

The periodic summary occurs at different times throughout a presentation to remind the listeners of the main points that have been stated.

A periodic summary can also serve as a transition from the previously stated main point to the next main point. A periodic summary is often employed when a presentation is long or the subject is complex.

The final summary takes place during the concluding remarks. It reviews all of the main points addressed during the entire presentation.

Let's examine an example of each of the three types of summaries:

1. The Preliminary Summary

Today my presentation will deal with the current recession I shall be addressing four main points: (1) major causes of the recession, (2) problems created by the recession, (3) viable options to correct the problems and (4) the solution I recommend for overcoming the recession.,

2. The Periodic Summary

So far today I have talked with you about two of the four main points that I'll be addressing. First, I shared some ideas on the causes of the recession and secondly, I stated my thoughts on the problems caused by it. Now, I'd like to identify several viable options for solving the problems.

3. The Final Summary

Today I've shared my ideas with you on four points closely related to the recession. I began by listing the causes of it (which were…). Next, I focused on the problems caused by it (such as…). My third main point identified possible options to correct the problems (which included…). And finally I offered what I consider to be the best solution for ending the recession.

Note the final summary should be brief and simply list the main points without any explanation.

USE VISUAL AIDS EFFECTIVELY

"Visual aids are one of the most powerful means
of amplification you have as a speaker"
- Joseph Devito

V isual aids are instructional and communications devices that appeal mainly to a listener's vision or sight. They include such things as: chalk boards, flip charts, films, slides, overheads, videos, charts, graphs, tables and photographs.

The use of visual aids enhances the meaning of the spoken word. They get results that words can't get by themselves because they provide a picture in the minds of the people listening. They are especially helpful to the numerous people who are visually oriented and use their eyes primarily to perceive and learn about things and events.

Visual aids should always serve as a definite purpose. They should not be employed as a gimmick or merely to fill time. Visuals should be used to clarify what you are saying and need to be synchronized with what you are saying at the time.

It is essential that when you are using a visual that you continue to look at and speak to your listeners rather than look at the aid itself (except for quick glances). It is also best to stand to the side of the visual instead of in front of it with your back to your listeners.

Seeing is not only believing it is an immense help to achieving understanding. There are several advantages to using visual aids when presenting information. Here are a few:

* creates and maintains interest
* clarifies information especially technical and statistical
* adds variety to the presentation
* assists with understanding and retention
* saves time
* emphasizes key points
* provides credibility to the data ("I saw it with my own eyes idea")

As we have seen, speakers can profit in many ways by using visual aids. However, unfortunately presenters often make mistakes when using them. You can use visuals properly and avoid making errors by following these recommended practices for preparing and delivering your talk:

First let's look at several tips for preparing your visual aids:

* make sure that the print and pictures are legible and large enough to be seen easily
* limit the amount of information you show on each visual (keep it uncluttered)
* use a simple and attractive layout and design
* employ plain lettering avoid script
* use brief headings for your main points
* separate the different points by either numbering them or by bullets
* highlight the most important information by contrasting colors, italics or underlining
* use several illustrations to break up the monotony of long lines of type
* double or triple space the typed material. Use plenty of white space in the margins and between the separate points
* explain the visual using only a few words and avoid long lines of type
* number the visuals to keep them in order

Now let's turn to a few ideas regarding using visual aids when presenting information:

* check out the room and seating arrangement ahead of time to ensure they are suitable for your talk, for example: electrical outlets, light dimmer switch, extension cords, extra bulbs for projectors, screen, tables to hold equipment, and lectern
* turn off the lights immediately in front of and behind the screen (leave all other lights on but dimmed)
* use a pointer to point to the information that you are talking about at the same time you are talking about it
* keep your visuals covered until you are actually referring to them (if you uncover them too early they will be a distraction to your listeners). Be sure to cover the visuals again as soon as you are finished talking about them.

In the event that you will be distributing handouts as a part of your presentation you would be wise to keep in mind that handouts can be both an asset and a liability. They can both save and waste time. They can focus attention on important information or they can prove to be distracting.

There are two major distraction problems involved with using handouts:

1. If distributed at the start of the presentation they can be distracting because people are likely to leaf through them right away and miss what is being said at the time
2. If distributed during your presentation they interrupt the flow of ideas and consume valuable time

Probably the best way to use handouts is to give each person a packet containing all the handouts (numbered) in the order of their presentation with the request that they keep the entire packet closed until you request them to look at a certain numbered handout. As you finish referring to the handout ask the listeners to close the packet promptly (note this request is not always honored).

Remember, many people have to see something to believe it. This is the advantage of using visuals competently.

ARTICULATE CAREFULLY

"Active and energetic articulation is
indispensable to good speech"
- John Irwin and Majorie Rosenberger

Articulation is the making and joining of separate sounds to make words. It is the clear and effective utterance of speech sounds. In addition, it is the crispness and precision with which we form words vocally. The word enunciation is used interchangeably with articulation.

Articulation occurs when the motion of the lips, tongue and velum together with the pulsation of the chest muscles and diaphragm produce the sounds of speech,.

Speech is basically an articulation process. Clear articulation is necessary to achieve understanding. Conversely, poor articulation interferes with getting understood and could make a person appear to be less intelligent than he/she really is.

Your goal should be to make each sound distinct, precise and easily intelligible. Try to attain a balance between overly precise and sloppy enunciation. Also strive to sound natural when you talk.

Clear articulation doesn't just happen. You need to make a concerted effort to produce the various sounds precisely and correctly.

You can significantly improve your articulation by doing the following:

* Become aware of the things you are doing wrong. You can do this by:

1. reading or talking aloud into a tape recorder and playing it back to learn how you sound to others
2. watching yourself on video tape or in the mirror as you speak
3. listening to especially articulate people to note how they speak and then comparing how they sound with how you sound
4. consulting a speech therapist to discover your faults and to get suggestions on how to overcome them

* make full use of your jaw, mouth, lips, tongue and face muscles in tandem with proper breath control
* open your lips wide when you speak and move your jaw freely up and down (avoid being lip lazy)
* relax your body and free it of tension especially your larynx or voice box
* improve your posture and breath control when talking
* keep your hands away from your mouth and chin while speaking
* produce each sound precisely by giving each vowel and consonant enough time (without sounding unnatural or stilted)
* say entire words without substituting, adding or dropping sounds (For example, talkin for talking often for ofen and sor, for saw)
* secure a list of tongue twister words and practice them to make your tongue more flexible and able to move more easily
* avoid mumbling or swallowing sounds because of insufficient mouth opening or a tight jaw

PRONOUNCE WORDS CORRECTLY

"Pronounce it faithfully" John Hay

Pronunciation is using the speech organ to produce words. It is how we say words.

Your pronunciation of words affects your listeners' understanding immensely. Listeners are distracted, and even irritated, when they hear words mispronounced. Worse yet, your image and credibility may suffer when you don't say words correctly and distinctly.

It is important to realizes that although most English words have only one correct pronunciation that many words have an alternate acceptable pronunciation. For example, the words either and route. In the final analysis, pronunciation patterns will be accepted if they coincide with those of the majority of educated people living in the community.

However, it is wise to use general (standard) American pronunciation. General American has fewer distinguishable speech characteristics than do regional pronunciations. The best pronunciation can't be identified with a certain geographical region such as Boston or Brooklyn. If you speak with a distinct dialect that is foreign to your listeners, you run the risk of setting yourself apart from them (whereas you really want to establish a feeling of commonality and togetherness with them).

The spelling of words in English is often different from the way they are pronounced. Thus, spelling can be misleading as far as correct pronunciation is concerned. Many words include a letter that is silent and should not be pronounced (For example often, salmon, entrepreneur, and indict).

On the other hand, some words include letters that should be pronounced but frequently are not. For example, February, library, poem and several. Still, other words are said incorrectly because a letter or syllable is wrongly added. For example: athalete, realitor, and idear.

A speaker's sloppiness or laziness when speaking accounts for additional mispronouncing of words. For example, thinkin for thinking, goin for going, ban for barn and ca for car.

You can improve your pronunciation in several ways such as:

* looking up how to pronounce new words or words you are uncertain about in a current dictionary (dictionaries list the most popular or common ways of pronouncing words). Better yet, consult a dictionary specializing in American pronouncing of words such as the one written by Kenyon and Knott.

* practicing pronouncing new words until you feel comfortable when saying them

* pronouncing a new word slowly syllable by syllable (a syllable is a single uttered sound).

* sounding natural when you pronounce words (don't draw attention to the way you say things by being overly precise or laboring with your pronunciation)

* speaking more slowly and distinctly when speaking to a group with different ethnic or cultural backgrounds

* refraining from adding sounds that say nothing when you are talking. For example, ah, um, and er

* substituting words that are easier to say when certain words give you trouble repeatedly. For example, use numbers instead of statistics

USE PAUSES WISELY

"I do not understand; I pause; I explain"
- Michael De Montaigne

A pause is a temporary stop a brief silence,. It is a short period of time when no words are uttered.

There are several benefits you can derive from using pauses effectively. These include:

* gives speaker a chance to think and thus present his/her thoughts in a more precise and organized manner
* provides listeners with time to digest the new ideas or complicated information just heard
* let's speaker appear to be carefully considering the next words he/she is going to utter
* allows speaker time to look carefully at his/her listeners to gain feedback from their reactions to what he/she has just said before proceeding to the next point
* permits the speaker to adjust his/her speaking style or content based on the feedback received
* emphasizes the importance of the point just made
* serves as a transition from one idea to the next
* creates suspense as to what the speaker is going to say next

The number and length of pauses should vary according to the speakers rate of speaking and the type of information being presented. For example, you may want to pause more frequently when sharing new, unfamiliar, or complicated information (or if you speak at a rapid pace)

In general, it is advisable to avoid too frequent or prolonged pauses. Unnatural pauses or undue hesitation can suggest to your listeners that you lack conviction or feel uncertain about what you are about to say.

In addition, you should try to eliminate the pauses caused by the use of ahs, ums, ers, you know and other filler sounds or words because they are meaningless, waste time and are distracting.

USE BODY LANGUAGE TO REINFORCE WORDS

"Trust not a man's words if you please, or you may
come to erroneous conclusions; but at all times
place implicit confidence in a man's countenance
in which there is no deceit"
- George Barrow

B ody language is the movement of any part of the body to
convey information as well as clarify and emphasize what
is being said. Body language together with voice tone constitute
a person's non-verbal communication.

Body language includes a person's facial expressions,
gestures, posture, movement of the head, shoulders, arms,
hands, legs, feet and torso.

Your body language plays an important role in your attempt
to gain understanding. For example, less than ten percent of
communication that deals with feelings and attitudes is
conveyed by words; the rest of the meaning comes from tone
or other non-verbal cues.

It is important to note that your body language:

* reflects your attitude and mental state intentionally or unintentionally
* enriches or detracts from your verbal message
* creates a reciprocal interaction with your listeners

In addition, your body language shows how you feel about (1) yourself, (2) your listeners and (3) what you are saying.

Your facial expressions and other body movements have a language of their own. It is important to realize that your non-verbal behavior receives more attention than your verbal message. Body language can strengthen, weaken or even contradict what you are saying. When your non-verbal language is consistent with your words it makes your message more clear and easy to understand. Conversely, when it is inconsistent it causes the message to be mixed and difficult to decipher.

While you are talking you will promote comprehension by using body language that is:

* natural and spontaneous
* purposeful rather than random
* coordinated and consistent with the words you're uttering at the time
* used judiciously rather than done to excess
* timed optimally with what is being said
* varied rather than repetitive
* employed to clarify, emphasize and reinforce the words being spoken

Try to refrain from using body language that is distracting and meaningless.

Since your body language is so important it is essential you analyze it. You need to know what your body is doing when speaking and how it is influencing your listeners. This is not easy to do because people are not typically aware of what their body is doing while they are talking. You can gain some valuable insights from:

* looking in a mirror while practicing your presentation
* video-taping sample behavior while speaking
* asking for objective feedback from people that you trust to tell you the truth

Understanding body language is difficult because it is extremely complicated and full of ambiguity. The same body language can be interpreted differently by different people at the same time. It's use and interpretation is strongly influenced by peoples: culture, prejudices, backgrounds etc. Body language also occurs in a certain context. The bottom line is that you need to be cautious about the body language you use when speaking and when attempting to read your listeners' body language.

SECURE CONTINUOUS FEEDBACK

"Men no longer test words to see what the truth
is in them, the majority are only interested
in knowing what their effect will be"
- Theodore Haecker

Feedback involves learning how effectively you have communicated. It is finding out how well your message has been understood. Feedback completes the communications loop between the sender (the speaker) and the receiver (the listener).

You can't merely assume that what you are saying is being understood. Therefore, it is necessary for you to verify that what you have actually said is what you intended to say and that your message has been heard as you intended it to be heard.

It is wise to give the obtaining of immediately feedback a high priority when communicating so that you can correct any misunderstandings as they occur. Feedback provides your listeners with the opportunity to make comments or ask questions about what you have said.

Fortunately, face-to-face communication furnishes you an excellent opportunity for securing instantaneous and continuous feedback from your listeners. Every listener sends out signals that disclose how your message is going over. These signals may be (1) verbal or non-verbal, (2) direct or indirect, or (3) conscious or unconscious (intentional or unintentional).

Let's examine some ways you can gain feedback:

* desiring to and actually working at getting it
* stating at the beginning of your talk that it is okay to interrupt you at any time to obtain clarification or more information. Also, make clear that there is no such thing as a dumb question and that is permissible to offer personal opinions and differing views.
* showing your appreciation for all questions asked and avoiding acting irritated with or defensive about any questions or comments
* maintaining steady eye contact with your listeners to learn their reactions as you speak
* noting the eye movements of your listeners (for example are they looking up or down, looking at you attentively or away from you with a bored look, or are their eyes alert or glazed over)
* observing facial expressions or a lack of them
* being aware of your listeners body posture (for example are they fidgeting or slouched over)
* watching movement of various parts of listeners bodies (for example, the hands and arms or legs and feet)
* asking people to repeat the essence of what you have said in their own words
* saying periodically "I know you have some questions, what are they?"
* pausing occasionally to give listeners time to digest especially important information while at the same time leaning forward and looking around with an expectant look on your face
* asking questions such as "What is your understanding of what I've just said?" or "What is your reaction to what I've just

spoken about?" or "What advantages and disadvantages can you see from what I've just proposed?"
  * responding to questions in an appreciative non-judgmental manner
  * refraining from asking questions such as:

1. "Do you understand what I have just said?"
2. "Do you agree with me that....?"
3. "What are your reasons for asking such a question?"

  * stating at the end of your comments that "Now is a good time to ask questions, however, if some questions come to mind later feel free to contact me about them"

SECTION 7
SPEAKING VOICE AND STYLE

AVOID DISTRACTING MANNERISMS

"For a man by nothing is so well
betrayed as by his manners"
- Edmund Spenser

A speaker's mannerisms are his/her adherence to a particular style or way of acting.

Try to avoid any distinctive mannerisms that distract from what you are saying. Your goal is to get your listeners to focus on your message rather than you as the messenger. A distraction is anything that interferes with the listeners ability to concentrate on what you are saying.

There are all kinds of speaker mannerisms that interfere with a listener's ability to give his/her full attention to what you are saying. These may be classified as (1) attitude, (2) voice, (3) style of delivery, (4) body movement and (5) use of language. Let's address each of these startling with attitude.

1. Attitude:

* acting either overly friendly (familiar) or detached (distant)

---

* acting superior or condescending
* acting too modest or humble
* coming across as a phony, unnatural or "trying too hard"
* appearing to be nervous, awed by or uncomfortable with the type of occasion or listeners

2. Voice:

* talking either too loudly or softly
* speaking with a rising inflection toward the end of sentences
* dropping volume at the end of sentences
* having a sing-song rhythm
* speaking with an unpleasant tone (For example, too shrill, husky or breathy)
* saying everything in a deadly monotone

3. Style of delivery:

* speaking either too fast or slow
* hesitating too long between sentences
* pausing awkwardly in the middle of sentences
* pronouncing words either too precisely or sloppily
* mispronouncing words or substituting sounds habitually (For example, Calyfornia for California, sor for saw or ca for car)
* providing unnecessary detail
* over or understating matters repeatedly
* stating things implicitly and indirectly rather than explicitly and directly
* overusing folksy and slang expressions
* stating all important information in a tentative manner that suggests a lack of confidence or competence

4. Body Movement:

* moving arms, hands, legs and feet excessively and randomly
* pacing around frequently without a purpose (like a caged lion)

* breathing deeply and sighing often
* shallow breathing causing a lack of breath at the end of sentences
* blinking eyes rapidly
* avoiding eye contact by looking up, down or away
* looking at listener's intently or slowly up and down their entire body
* closing eyes for a prolonged period of time especially during pauses
* taking glasses on and off repeatedly
* playing with eye glasses or looking over the top of them
* smacking or licking lips while speaking
* talking with hand on chin and barely moving of the lips
* moving arms and gesturing in an aimless repetitive fashion
* messaging hands or arms, pulling on an ear, or rubbing of nose
* making a pyramid of hands while making an important point and then speaking behind the pyramid
* moving hands and fingers nervously (For example, shuffling papers, tapping with a pen, playing with coins or jewelry or with buttons on clothing)
* touching listeners bodies frequently when talking to them

5. Use of Language:

* repeating certain words and phrases excessively. (For example, you know, like, whatever, awesome, and I have to tell you this)
* making frequent and blatant grammatical errors
* using tired and worn out phrases such as "It doesn't take a rocket scientist to know..."
* using fancy language to impress rather than express
* using several words when one would suffice and long complex sentences when shorter and simpler ones would be adequate

ACT NATURAL

"What is natural is never disgraceful" Euripedes

When people act natural they are real, genuine and authentic. They don't disguise or hide who they really are. A speaker is real when he/she talks naturally and sounds like him/her self. You must be genuine to truly communicate. When you are speaking you are continually sending signals (by your words, attitudes and actions) that reveal who and what you are.

Your goal is to have your listeners view you as a genuine person who is a straight talker and who can be trusted.

People need to trust you and believe that you are credible before they are able to believe what you say to them.

Listeners respect and admire speakers who have the courage to act natural and who are free of any affectation. Conversely, listeners are suspicious and resent speakers who are phonies and try to "fake it".

You can convey that you are sincere, natural and real in several ways including:

* demonstrating a sense of being secure and not acting defensive

* disclosing some personal things about yourself that show your listeners that you are willing to let them know the real you
* showing the strength of your convictions by displaying some emotion while talking about a subject
* using words and phrases that you normally use
* gesturing frequently, freely and spontaneously
* speaking with a voice tone that matches your real feelings and views about your topic
* matching your facial expressions and body language with what is being uttered
* looking and acting relaxed and comfortable

BE DIRECT

"Many times it is effective and easy to begin
with an immediate reference to your subject"
- John Irwin and Majorie Rosenberger

When you speak in a direct manner you go from one point to the next in the shortest way without any deviation. You get right to the point and stick to the crux of the matter being discussed.

Being direct also involves speaking the truth and stating your real thoughts and feelings. It is being straightforward and forthright.

There is another dimension to being direct that influences getting understood. It is talking directly to the person(s) that you want to receive your message. You deliberately bypass intermediary or third parties.

You avoid rambling, taking detours and hedging your comments when you are direct. And you don't merely hint or imply something when talking with people. You say what is on your mind.

By knowing and stating your purpose you are better able to limit your comments to those directly related to your purpose.

It is worth noting that being direct with someone is not always a good idea. Being direct with the wrong person or at the wrong time can backfire and cause problems. For example, various cultures and personality types are not equally comfortable with and may even resent talk that is direct. In addition, speaking about sensitive issues directly may embarrass people and cause them to be annoyed and reject what you are telling them.

People speak indirectly when they don't say exactly what they mean. Obviously, when people speak indirectly they risk being misunderstood and being perceived as evasive.

When something needs to be said it is usually best to come right out and say it in a straightforward manner. You can't assume that people know what you think or feel about a matter-you need to tell them.

When being direct it is important to restrict your comments to the essence of the problem. The essence of crux of a problem includes these factors:

* defining the problem precisely
* assessing the magnitude or severity of the problem
* determining how long the problem has existed and whether it has been getting better or worse
* identifying the causes or triggering events
* identifying the people contributing to the problem
* uncovering possible options or solutions
* choosing the best solution

Here are several tips for getting directly to the point:

* keep your introduction and conclusion short
* talk about only one thing at a time
* cut out any unnecessary words
* use short words and sentences
* minimize small talk and irrelevant comments
* give the supporting material for your main point immediately after stating your point
* stop talking once you have made your point

GET TO AND STICK TO THE POINT

"But still remember, if you mean to please, to press your point with modesty and ease"
- William Cowper

To get straight to the point means you immediately begin talking about the crux or essence of a matter. To stick to a point means you talk strictly and exclusively about matters relevant to the topic being discussed at the time.

Effective speakers get directly to the point and stick to it until all that needs to be said gets said. Your goal is to get the most out of a presentation in the least amount of time. You achieve this by concentrating on only one topic at a time, limiting comments to only relevant points and refraining from discussing whatever happens to come to mind at the time.

One effective way to get right to the point is to immediately state your purpose and then proceed directly to your first main point. In addition, it is wise to avoid having a lengthy introduction or offering excessive background information.

People are busy and are bombarded with heaps of information constantly. Therefore, they prefer and appreciate it when you get right to the crux of the subject. Conversely, they object and resent it when you waste time by taking all day to get to the essence of your presentation.

The crux or essence of a matter deals directly with the purpose of your talk. The crux of a problem involves three things:

1. a precise and clear description of the problem
2. causes of the problem
3. viable solutions to the problem

Now let's examine several important aspects of sticking to the point. Anything discussed should be (1) important and worthwhile, (2) directly related to the topic, (3) make a difference and (4) contribute to the discussion.

Regrettably, managing to get people to speak only about the matter currently being discussed is a constant battle because people like to ramble, digress, and go off on tangents. They typically have difficulty disciplining themselves by limiting their comments to the subject at hand.

These approaches have been found to be effective in helping people to stick to the point:

* set and agree upon ground rules for the discussion (the do's and don'ts)
* identify and clearly state the purpose of the discussion
* minimize conjecture, speculation, and stating mere opinion
* avoid excessive details, endless examples, and long explanations
* forbid "war stories" and all other interesting but irrelevant anecdotes
* focus on the present and future and not the past
* use a flip chart or chalk board to list key ideas/points stated to provide focus to aid retention
* challenge in a definite but respectful manner anything being said that has been said before or that appears to be off target
* stop promptly when nothing new is being said

Another effective approach to keeping on target is to put these questions on a flip chart or overhead projector in front of the group you are addressing to guide your discussion:

1. What are we doing right?
2. What do we need to do better?
3. What do we need to do differently?
4. What do we need to do faster or slower?
5. What do we need to do more or less of?
6. What do we need to stop doing?

When problem solving focusing on these questions will aid the discussion by helping you to stick to the point.

* what exactly is the problem?
* what is the scope and seriousness of the problem?
* how long has the problem existed? (Is it getting better or worse?)
* when does the problem occur or what condition or events appear to trigger the problem?
* what appear to be the major causes of the problem?
* who appears to be involved in the problem and to what extent?
* what appears to be the consequences of the problem if it were to continue?
* what options are available for solving the problem?
* how can the solution chosen be implemented most effectively?

SPEAK WITH AN EFFECTIVE STYLE

"Proper words in proper places marks
the true definition of style"
- Jonathan Swift

A speaker's style is his/her distinctive manner of expressing him/herself while speaking. It is the speaker's particular manner of saying or doing something. Speaking style includes such behaviors as:

* rate of speaking
* type of body movements

* confident-assured appearance
* personal vs. impersonal comments
* use of notes and aids
* voice variations

* direct vs. indirect statements
* formal vs. informal way of talking
* assertive vs. non-assertive demeanor
* degree of listener involvement
* flexible vs. inflexible attitude
* way uses visual aids

Your communicating style affects your listeners receptivity to what you are telling them. When a speaking style differs markedly from that which his/her listeners are comfortable with misunderstanding frequently occurs. Your listeners react to both what you say and how you say it. However, it is important for you to realize that how people say things (style) is generally more important than what they say (substance) as far as your listeners are concerned.

There is no one style that is recommended for all speakers. Your listeners, the subject and the occasion all call for different speaking styles and approaches. You need to develop a speaking style that you are comfortable with and that works for you. And although it is best for you to develop your own style it is worth noting that generally an informal, friendly, and open style is favored by most listeners.

Bottomline-any style that helps you to say what you want to say and that assists your listeners to understand what you are saying is the right style for you to use.

Factors that affect a speaker's style are:

* purpose for speaking
* type of situation or occasion
* subject and content
* time available for presenting
* type of seating arrangement (eg. classroom or circular)
* kind of setting and size of room
* type of listeners
* number of people present
* personality of speaker
* presenters speaking skills and experience
* type and amount of instructional aids to be used

Here are several ways that you can develop an effective speaking style:

* observe the speaking styles of people who are effective speakers so that you become aware of what they do and don't do (but don't copy another person's style)
* analyze your own speaking style by watching videos and listening to tapes of yourself speaking on various subjects

* ask for feedback from people who have heard you speak and who are willing to be frank with you (you can also pass out evaluation forms to your listeners at the conclusion of your presentations)

* develop your own distinct style that is natural and comfortable for you one that permits your personality to come through

* adapt your speaking style based on the listeners, subject and occasion

* speak enthusiastically and in a conversational manner for most speaking occasions

* use lively language that appeals to your listeners

* practice speaking to develop and refine your skills (practice with different kinds of content as well as different rates of speaking)

* consult with a speech expert to obtain the basics of effective speaking and read recommended literature addressing the fundamentals of public speaking (For example, Dale Carnegie's book)

* join a toast master's club

* avoid any annoying or distracting mannerisms such as: repetitive hand and arm movements, habitual facial expressions, and pacing around like a caged animal

USE THE RIGHT RATE OF SPEAKING

"You should speak as rapidly as you can be
clearly and comfortably understood"
- Kenneth McFarland

Your speaking rate is the speed or pace at which you speak. It is the number of words you speak within a certain time limit-usually the number of words spoken per minute.

There are three factors that determine your rate of speaking:

1. type of subject matter (the content)
2. time available for you to speak
3. listeners knowledge and interest in the topic

Strive to attain a happy medium between speaking too fast or too slow. It is unwise to say too much too fast. Conversely, if you talk too slowly you will bore your listeners and lose their attention.

There is no single ideal rate of speaking. The general rule is to speak as rapidly as you comfortably can while still saying your words clearly and getting what you are saying understood.

It is normally best to speak at a moderate rate with a conversational style. People usually speak between 120-150 words per minute. You should try to speak at a rate of at least 120 words per minute. If you speak too fast your listeners may view your speaking as impersonal and that you are unconcerned about your ability to be understood (it is worth nothing that few speakers speak too fast to be understood because the average listener can understand at a rate far faster than the average speaker can speak). Conversely, try to never speak slower than 100 words per minute or your listeners understanding will suffer.

Proper pauses can enhance understanding, whereas inappropriate pauses can create problems. Refrain from pausing in the middle or a thought group instead wait until the end of the thought group. Try to avoid prolonged pauses because they can interrupt the continuity of what you are saying; they can also suggest that you are uncertain about the next thing you want to say.

Proper pauses can be a huge plus. For example, they can:

* emphasize your main points
* give listeners time to reflect on what you've said
* allow time for listeners to make comments or ask questions
* serve as a transition between the last and next point
* provide you time to organize your thoughts and search for the exact word you want to say next
* (please note for more details on the use of the pause refer to the pause section of this book)

The following ideas should help you to speak at an effective rate:

* speak more slowly when stating your key points to emphasize them and let them sink in
* speak more slowly when introducing new or especially difficult information

* talk at a faster rate when presenting details and less important information
* state information familiar to listeners more quickly
* vary your pace to maintain interest
* speak at a rate that feels comfortable to you and that permits you to pronounce each word distinctly
* determine your speaking rate by timing yourself preferably with a stop watch for a minute at a time. Do this for the different kinds of content (write down the times to refer to later)
* practice speaking until you are speaking at the desired rate
* time and record the times for each practice session (and do this for each major section of your talk)

HAVE AN APPEALING MESSAGE
AND VOICE TONE

"Susceptible people are more affected by a change
in tone than by unexpected words"
- George Elliot

The tone of a message expresses its attitudes, mood or the emotions involved as revealed by its wording. Tone is hard to define precisely. It is an intangible that creates a certain feeling in the people listening to you. Your words can send one message and your voice something entirely different. For example, when a person who has just received bad news says "wonderful" or "great" with a serious and depressed tone of voice.

Your tone, or the overall feelings conveyed by your message, provides insights into your personality and your attitude toward your listeners and subject. The tone also discloses your "in between the lines" thinking about something.

A positive tone to a message is generally preferable to a negative one. A positive tone sounds cheerful, pleasant and upbeat. On the other hand, a negative tone sounds pessimistic, skeptical and full of doubt.

Word things in a positive tone whenever you can. Listeners respond more favorably to positive messages. Positive messages encourage understanding whereas negative messages encourage misunderstanding.

Negative words that you should avoid using include: no, won't, can't, impossible, fault, blame, wrong, disagreement, and foolish. Why? Because they frequently trigger an unfavorable reaction.

Let's look at a couple of examples of positive (P) and negative (N) ways of saying things:

1. (P) An employee enthusiastically presents an idea to his/her boss which elicits this response "Thanks for your suggestion I appreciate it. Let's see if we can find a way to use your idea."

(N) "so, you have still another idea huh? The problem with your idea is that it is impractical-why don't you get back to work?"

2. (P) A fellow is discussing the United State's chances in the Olympic games with a friend and says "I can't wait to see the Olympic Games on TV. I think we have an excellent chance to win the most gold medals because our athletes are much improved from the last games."

(N) I may watch the games on TV if there is nothing better to do. I'd like to see the Americans do well, but I don't have much hope because our athletes never seem to be in peak condition.

It is advisable to tone your message in the way that is most appropriate for conveying that particular kind of information to a certain person or group.

Normally, a friendly warm tone to a message is more desirable than an impersonal cold one. The message tone should sound sincere and hopeful. It should always sound as though you are talking to an equal and never sound superior or condescending.

You will create a more favorable tone to your message if you frequently use you, we and us and rarely say I, me, and my when speaking with people.

Now, let's turn to how voice tone influences the reception of what you say to people.

Your tone of voice is important in setting the tone of your overall message. Your voice tone can give multiple meaning to what you are saying. For example, if you are talking about something serious your voice tone should be solemn and deep. However, if you are saying something light and frivolous your voice tone should have a lighter and lively tone to it.

Speak in a confident tone of voice to make a good impression on people, however beware of sounding cocky, superior or demanding as this kind of voice tone alienates people and causes them to react negatively toward both you and your message. Also try to avoid habitually speaking with either a dull bored sounding voice or a high pitched excitable sounding voice.

Typically, people are unaware of their voice tone and how it affects others. Sometimes they may be aware that something about their voice tone is causing a negative reaction and yet not have a clue as to what specifically is provoking such a negative reaction. It is vital to your success as a speaker (and as a person) that you pin down the exact nature of the problem.

There are several things you can do to analyze our voice tone:

1. tape your voice and listen to it as attentively and objectively as possible
2. ask your friends and co-workers to give you honest and frank feedback on how your voice sounds to them (when you do this be sure to express your appreciation for their candor and help)
3. consult with a speech specialist at a university or in private practice for his/her reactions and advice
4. consider your total personality, your basic attitudes toward life and your relationships with people to gain additional insight.

It is wise to pay close attention to your voice tone because it reveals who you really are.

SPEAK WITH A PLEASANT VOICE QUALITY

"So smooth, so sweet is they voice" Robert Herrick

Voice quality is the overall sound of a person's voice. It is the combined characteristics of a voice that makes it pleasant or unpleasant to listen to. Voice quality includes: the basic tone, pitch levels, resonance, clarity and articulation.

Your voice is you. People judge you by the way you sound. Your voice quality is of prime importance in determining the impression you make on the people listening to you. Your voice should reflect the real you. It is the mirror of your basic personality, physical state and mood at the time. Since your voice quality is so important it is imperative that you gain insights into whether your listeners consider your voice to be pleasant or unpleasant.

Your listeners want to listen to a person with a pleasant sounding voice that is free of annoying or distracting features. There is no doubt that people are more receptive to what you say when they like your voice and more resistant to your message when they don't like the sound of your voice.

Your goal should be to develop a pleasant, warm and expressive voice. A pleasant voice originates from a relaxed chest, wide open lips and a relaxed throat and neck. It has a clarity and purity of tone. In addition, the pitch level is neither too high nor too low.

A pleasant voice is free from breathiness and hoarseness and it has neither too much nor too little nasal sound. Let's examine three key ingredients of voice quality: (1) breathing, (2) resonance and (3) pitch:

1. Breathing
    Proper breathing is essential to good voice quality and projection. The source of energy for producing sound is the breath stream. Breath for speaking originates in the diaphragm. Speech occurs as breath is exhaled (your diaphragm supports your breath and your breath supports your voice.)
    Your breath exhalation needs to be controlled, steady and adequate. Your inhalation needs to be quick enough to avoid interrupting the continuity of your words. A sip of air is all that you need to utter long phrases. Whenever you inhale be sure to do it silently without any tension in your neck or throat.
    Breathe often so that you will always have an ample reserve behind your vocal cords. If you run out of air your volume at the end of sentences will be diminished and you may even drop your entire sentence endings. Your voice sounds old, weak and tired when it is not supported by adequate air.

2. Resonance
    Resonance is the vibration of the vocal cords which then set the air within the resonators into vibration. The resonators determine the quality of your voice tone. A deeply resonant voice adds to the richness of the voice sound and is pleasant to listen to (For example, Tom Brokaw and Chris Wallace.)
    The resonators modify and amplify the sound waves produced by the vocal cords. The main resonators are: (1) the throat, (2) the mouth and (3) the nasal cavities. You can improve the resonance of your voice by:

    * singing
    * imitating the voices of radio and television announcer whose tone and resonance you admire

* practicing lowering and deepening your voice tone and listening to how you sound on tape

3. Pitch

Pitch refers to both voice range and inflection. The range is the difference between the highest and lowest pitch levels. Inflection is the pitch changes that make a voice interesting to listen to. Pitch is determined by the frequency of the vibrations of your vocal folds as you push air through them.

Strive to speak at a low pitch level most of the time. However, your pitch level should vary according to what you are saying at the time (more details regarding pitch are dealt with in the voice variety section of this book)

Fortunately, there are many ways you can improve the quality of your voice. It can definitely be improved with proper training and practice. However, you will need to make a strong commitment and concerted effort to improve it. It won't be easy nor will it happen instantly. By practicing recommended techniques you can improve: pitch level, volume, rate, variety and overall quality of your speaking voice.

To improve your voice quality:

* enroll in a public speaking course
* join the Toastmasters Club in your area
* secure and study videos of effective speaking and speakers
* read an introductory speech text to acquaint yourself with the basic do's and don'ts
* record your voice on audio tape and listen critically to how you sound (identify your strengths and weaknesses and jot them down for reference)
* ask your friends and business associates, who are willing to be frank with you, if they have noted any annoying voice mannerisms
* speak with your natural voice unless it has defects
* speak with a smooth flowing rhythm and pace
* talk with a moist empty mouth
* articulate distinctly-practice tongue twister exercises until you have mastered them (to improve tongue flexibility)

* maintain a correct posture to aid your breathing and to feel relaxed (sit and stand tall-don't slouch)

* increase control of your breathing and air flow by breathing from deep within your diaphragm

* breathe silently with quick silent sips of air (especially if you are using a microphone)

* keep your hands away from your jaw and mouth when talking

* find and speak at your optimal pitch level

* make proper use of your articulators

* open your mouth wide and move your lips freely

* relax and open your throat to minimize tension and encourage sufficient projection of your voice

USE VOICE VARIETY

"The voice so sweet, the words so fair, as some soft
chime had stroked the air" Ben Jonson

Voice variety includes speaking with different sounds or
changes in the voice. You achieve vocal variety by
changes in: volume, tone, and pitch level.

Voice variety is a must. Unless you vary your voice you will
bore your listeners because you will be speaking without
enthusiasm and in a monotone.

There are several important reasons to vary your voice
when speaking such as:

* creates interest
* holds peoples attention
* emphasizes certain ideas and facts
* expresses speakers attitude and feelings at the time
* promotes listener understanding

Any sentence can be said in a variety of ways by varying the
rate, volume and pitch level. It is a good idea to experiment
with each of these factors to ascertain what works best for you.

We have addressed voice loudness and tone as well as
speaking rate in previous sections of this book. However, not

much has been stated about pitch so far. Therefore let's now examine the various aspects of pitch in more detail.

Pitch refers to both range and inflection. As mentioned previously, range is the difference between the highest and lowest pitch levels and inflection is the pitch changes, up and down, of your voice when speaking.

You need to vary your pitch optimally to be effective as a speaker. Changes in pitch level enable you to convey your feelings about a subject or situation. An expressive and lively voice requires pitch variations. An effective speaker's pitch level moves up and down continuously in an infinite variety of patterns much like a musical scale. It is best to use both high and low notes as appropriate, but use the in-between notes most of the time.

Speak with a high pitch level to express excitement, enthusiasm and light heartedness. Speak with a low pitch level to express confidence and solemnity. The best pitch level to use depends on the nature of the subject and the type of occasion.

Most people prefer to listen to a pleasant low pitched (keyed) voice. On the other hand, they dislike listening to a high pitched voice because this can be irritating and distracting. The use of a higher pitch at the end of a sentence can change a statement into a question and suggest uncertainty and a lack of confidence. In contrast, a habitual downward pitch can appear to be dogmatic and even aggressive. The habitual use of either too high or too low a pitch is ill advised.

Each person has an optimal pitch. This is the level at which the person's voice performs at its best. It is the tone that is most rich, full and resonant. Your optimal pitch is the one that is most comfortable for you and the one you speak in the most.

You can attain vocal variety by:

* varying the loudness and softness of your voice
* changing the pitch level based on the kind of words being spoken and the feelings the speaker has while saying the words
* varying the quality of the voice (for example, stern to gentle)

Please note that the method of identifying your optimal pitch level is beyond the scope of this book, but may be determined by consulting any good book on the fundamentals of public speaking.

SPEAK WITH SUFFICIENT VOICE LOUDNESS

"Lo, he doth send out his voice, yea,
and that a mighty voice"
- Book of Common Prayer

V oice loudness has to do with its intensity of sound or its volume. It refers to audibility. It ranges from an extremely loud to an extremely low sound.

Your listeners can't understand what they can't hear. Your goal is to speak neither too loudly nor too softly. You need to speak loud enough to be heard easily yet not so loud that it is offensive. The loudness of your voice should vary according to:

* the subject you are talking about
* the size and acoustics of the room you're speaking in
* the number of people listening to you
* the type of seating arrangement
* the surrounding noise and types of distractions
* whether or not you are using a microphone

It is important to realize three things about your voice volume:

1. your voice sounds louder to you than it does to others because it reverberates inside your head
2. your listeners are more likely to tune you out if you speak too softly than they are to strain to hear what you are saying
3. a loud voice is necessary for you to succeed as a speaker. For example, a loud voice makes you sound more confident and credible.

To create and maintain sufficient volume you need to:

* breathe deeply from your diaphragm to fill your lungs with adequate air so you can project your voice powerfully
* open your mouth enough to increase your resonance
* open your mouth wide to speak without any obstructions
* move your lips freely; avoid lazy lips
* keep your mouth moist while speaking
* stand or sit with an alert posture as you can breathe more easily
* keep your hands away from your jaw and mouth so you won't stifle your words
* remove gum or any other substance from your mouth while speaking
* face your listeners constantly when speaking
* record your normal speaking voice to discover how you sound to others (you don't sound the same to other people as you do to yourself)
* test your speaking or microphone loudness to determine if everyone in the room can hear you easily (ask the people in the back of the room to raise their hands if they can hear you easily and ask the people up front if you are talking too loud)
* refrain from letting your voice trail off or fade at the end of your sentences

APPENDIX A

SELF-ASSESSMENT OF GETTING WHAT YOU SAY UNDERSTOOD SKILLS

Instructions: please check the one column that best describes your attitude, knowledge and action for each factor listed:

Always = A Usually = U Rarely = R Never = N

	A	U	R	N
1. I think about what I am going to say before I say something				
2. When communicating I share complete, current and accurate information with people				
3. I share information in a timely manner				
4. I adapt the content of my message to the kind of people I am talking with				
5. I adapt my style of talking to the kind of people I am talking with				
6. I pronounce my words clearly, carefully and correctly				

7. My attitude and actions show that I like and respect people				
8. I am aware of the needs and feelings of the people I talk with				
9. My body language, voice tone and words are consistent and all send the same message to people				
10. My statements are brief and directly to the point without sounding abrupt				
11. I say things in a candid, forthright and straightforward manner				
12. I say things briefly without omitting important information				
13. I strive to achieve commonality and a sense of togetherness when talking with people				
14. I say things in a concrete and specific a way as I possibly can				
15. I have the courage to say things that need to be said to people honestly without toning it down				
16. I am aware of and respect the cultural differences among the people I talk with				
17. I use familiar and commonly used words and avoid technical terms when speaking with people				
18. I make a sincere and definite effort to get understood by people				
19. I have and show empathy for the people that I communicate with				
20. I emphasize the most important content when talking with people				

20. I emphasize the most important content when talking with people				
21. I am enthusiastic when conversing with people				
22. I use frequent and relevant examples when explaining things to people				
23. I have realistic expectations for getting what I say understood				
24. I say things in an explicit way to people				
25. I use gender neutral and fair language when talking with people				
26. I seek prompt feedback to ensure that what I said was understood				
27. I use correct grammar when speaking with people				
28. I limit the amount of information that I share with people at any one time				
29. I make a consistent and definite effort to say things in an interesting manner				
30. I realize people have short attention spans and that I need to work to retain their attention				
31. I know that I must show an interest in the people listening to me for them to want to listen to me				
32. I avoid having mannerisms when speaking that are distracting or annoying to people				
33. I act genuine and natural when interacting with people				

34. I share my thoughts in an organized manner and in a logical sequence				
35. I get directly to the point and stick to it when speaking with people				
36. I use precise words and say exactly what I intend to say to people				
37. I know and state my specific purpose for talking with people about important matters				
38. I establish rapport quickly with the people I am talking with				
39. I vary my rate of speaking depending on the type of content and people listening to me				
40. I include only important information and omit unimportant information when talking with people				
41. I repeat information with different words to help me get understood				
42. I use simple words and plain language when speaking with people				
43. I am sincere and demonstrate my sincerity when I say something				
44. I summarize important points when talking at length on a topic				
45. I am both tactful and truthful when I talk with people				
46. I select the best time for both me and others when I am going to talk with them about important matters				
47. I make clear and definite transitions when going from point to point when speaking about something important				

48. I speak loud enough for people to hear me easily				
49. I try to develop a large vocabulary so that I can express myself more exactly				
50. I realize that words have different meanings to different people and act accordingly when talking with people				

SCORING INSTRUCTIONS: check to see that you have answered all 50 questions. Give yourself 4 points for every always answer, 3 points for usually, 2 points for rarely and 1 for never. Add up all your points.

SCORING SCALE
180-200 points = excellent 160-179 = superior
140-159 = satisfactory 0-139 = unsatisfactory

MY TOTAL POINTS = MY SCORE =

APPENDIX B

SELF-ASSESSMENT OF GETTING WHAT IS SAID TO YOU UNDERSTOOD SKILLS

Instructions: please check the one column that best describes your attitude, knowledge and action for each factor listed:

Always = A Usually = U Rarely = R Never = N

	A	U	R	N
1. I avoid letting a person's appearance distract me from what they are saying				
2. I give my full attention to what peole are saying to me				
3. I have an open-minded and receptive attitude about what a person is saying to me				
4. I am aware that the same word can have different meanings to different people				
5. I avoid pre-judging or jumping to conclusions regarding what people are saying to me				

6. I observe the body language of people to help me understand what they are saying				
7. I read between the lines to help me understand what a person is really saying				
8. I listen carefully to identify the main ideas being stated by a person				
9. I distinguish between fact, inference and opinion when a person is talking to me				
10. I encourage people to speak candidly with me				
11. When something is said that is unclear to me I ask questions to clarify what the person has said				
12. I am alert to the mixed signals conveyed by the person speaking to me				
13. I make a strong effort to understand what a person is saying to me				
14. I study the context in which a statement is made to help me understand what it means				
15. I listen objectively to what people say to me				
16. I ask the person speaking to define unfamiliar words or technical terms for me				
17. I consider the cultural background of the person speaking when interpreting what they are saying				
18. I ask people to explain things they say to me so that I can understand them				

19. I avoid being distracted by a person's inflammatory or highly emotional language				
20. I realize that I can absorb only a limited amount of information at one time				
21. I recognize my emotional blind spots and prejudices regarding people, beliefs and things				
22. I avoid discussing important matters when I am preoccupied, tired or not feeling well				
23. I avoid taking mental vacations or tuning people out when they are talking with me				
24. I pay special attention to a speaker's introductory and concluding comments when listening to a presentation				
25. I do my best to maintain interest in what people are saying to me				
26. I notice whether the person speaking habitually uses words that overstate or understate things				
27. I try to learn the purpose or why a person is discussing a particular subject with me				
28. I identify the speaker's transitions as he/she moves from one topic to the next				
29. I pay more attention to a speaker's content than to his/her style of speaking				
30. I allocate adequate time to discuss important matters with people				

31. I listen to a person's voice tone as well as the content of what he/she is saying to me				
32. I have developed a large vocabulary to help me understand what is said to me				
33. I pay close attention to a speaker's choice of words				
34. I notice when people use words that qualify their meaning by being vague or self-protective				
35. I avoid being unduly influenced by the quality of a person's voice				
36. I attempt to determine the credibility and sincerity of the people I talk with				
37. I select a private and quiet place to hold important discussions				
38. I avoid being unduly influenced by a speaker's big words and fancy language				
39. I have the courage to let people be frank and level with me				
40. I look up the meaning of new words when I hear them				
41. I try to determine if a speaker's information is current, complete and accurate				
42. I try to identify the biases and motivations of people I talk with				
43. I sit or stand in an alert but comfortable position when discussing something important				

44. I know my listening strengths and weaknesses				
45. I ask people to get to and stick to the point when they start to ramble				
46. I avoid letting a persons use of incorrect grammar distract me from hearing what they are saying				
47. I help people I am talking with to relax and feel at ease				
48. I notice when the person speaking pauses, changes pitch level, the volume or rate of speaking				
49. I provide prompt and ongoing feedback while I listen to a person talking				
50. I listen closely to the total person (words, voice tone and body language) to help me understand what is being said				

SCORING INSTRUCTIONS: check to see that you have answered all 50 questions. Give yourself 4 points for every always answer, 3 points for usually, 2 points for rarely and 1 for never. Add up all your points.

SCORING SCALE
180-200 points = excellent   160-179 points = superior
140-159 points = satisfactory 0-139 point = unsatisfactory

MY TOTAL POINTS =   MY SCORE =